SEVEN KINGS
OF ENGLAND

NON FICTION BOOKS BY GEOFFREY TREASE

Biography

THE SEVEN QUEENS OF ENGLAND
THE SEVEN KINGS OF ENGLAND
SEVEN STAGES

History

THE ITALIAN STORY (Macmillan)
THIS IS YOUR CENTURY

CHARLES I

SEVEN KINGS
OF ENGLAND

by

GEOFFREY TREASE

Illustrated by

LESLIE ATKINSON

HEINEMANN : LONDON

William Heinemann Ltd
LONDON MELBOURNE TORONTO
CAPE TOWN AUCKLAND

First published 1955
Reprinted 1958, 1966

Printed in Great Britain
by Bookprint Limited
Kingswood, Surrey

Contents

List of Illustrations

Foreword

THE particular seven kings in this book have been chosen
for the dramatic quality in their lives and the interest (though
not always the excellence) of their characters. After that I
have considered variety of period: this mixed bag includes a
Saxon and a Norman, an early Plantagenet and a late one, and
then a trio of Stuarts, whose reigns make three acts in one
continuous play. There are no Tudors, but their family was
well represented in the previous volume, *The Seven Queens of
England*, to which this book comes as a companion.

Again I am indebted to innumerable histories and bio-
graphies which I have consulted for this fact or that, and
it is only possible here to list the chief works that have helped
me: *Alfred the Great, The Truth Teller*, B. A. Lees; *A History
of the Anglo-Saxons*, R. H. Hodgkin; *Anglo-Saxon England*, Sir
Frank Stenton; *William the Conqueror*, E. A. Freeman; *William
the Conqueror*, H. Belloc; *Richard the Lion Heart*, K. Norgate;
Coeur de Lion, C. A. Wilkinson; *Edward IV*, L. Stratford; *The
Life and Reign of Edward the Fourth*, C. L. Scofield; *Charles 1*,
Evan John; *Charles, King of England, King Charles and King
Pym*, and *King Charles the Martyr*, all by E. Wingfield Stratford;
Charles II, A. Bryant; *William III*, H. D. Traill.

Acknowledgment is also made to Messrs. A. D.
Peters, agents of the late H. Belloc for permission to
quote from his poem "The Ballad of Val-ès-Dunes",
published by Messrs. Duckworth in his *Sonnets and
Verses*.

1

Alfred: The Shepherd of the English

On a certain day in the middle of the ninth century, in Rome, a small English boy—he was about four—was solemnly arrayed in the robes and ceremonial belt of a consul.

That boy was destined to become King of England. He was, in fact, to be one of the greatest who have ever borne that title, and the first whose name is still familiar to us. And he was, it is fairly safe to suppose, the only Roman consul who was ever an English king as well.

In one sense it did not mean much when Pope Leo IV conferred the empty rank of consul on the small boy Alfred from Wessex. It was hundreds of years since real power had rested with Roman consuls such as Julius Cæsar and Pompey. In the ninth century A.D. the title was just a picturesque survival—or revival—like the phrase "Holy Roman Emperor" to describe the great Frankish king, Charlemagne, a generation earlier. The real Roman Empire had splintered centuries ago.

But, in another sense, that ceremony in Rome did mean something.

The little boy came from an England of green woods and bare green hills. He was born in the shadow of the chalk downs at Wantage, in Berkshire, and all his childhood was spent in timber-built country manors or in miniature towns of a few thousand inhabitants, scarcely more than the large villages of today. His world was one of horses and hounds, of birds singing in the branches and fish leaping in the unsullied streams.

He had come to a city which had once held between a million and a million and a half people. The population might have fallen since the great days of the Empire, but the buildings remained. New walls had just been raised to protect the city, and those walls linked no fewer than forty-four towers. Rome lived on under the Popes, still the centre and the wonder of the world. Classical ruins stood side by side with Christian churches, monasteries, and shrines. Even the most pious pilgrim gaped in wonder at the remains of the pagan amphitheatre, and murmured the familiar tag:

> "*When falls the Colosseum, Rome shall fall,*
> *And when Rome falls, the world.*"

All his life long, Alfred was to look back upon the glories of Roman civilisation as models—not just to be copied, but to be adapted to English needs. Law, learning, literature, the Latin language: those were the civilised heritage, those were what some day he was to seek for his own people.

Roman consul, King of England . . . Memories of past greatness, foundations of greatness in the future . . .

The little boy, smiling up at the Pope, proudly fingering his wonderful new belt, can be seen now as a link between two epochs in history.

Alfred did not talk to Leo, except through interpreters, for no Pope could be expected to converse in English, and Alfred was a grown man before he managed to learn Latin.

But if Leo did put to him the usual questions that old gentlemen put to small boys, in this case with someone to translate them, he would have learnt that Alfred's illustrious father, King Ethelwulf of Wessex, was well, and hoped to make the pilgrimage to Rome himself next year or the year after, if the Danish pirates did not become too active in the meantime; that Alfred was "the baby of the family", having three brothers, Ethelbald, Ethelbert, and Ethelred, and a sister, Ethelswith, who had just gone off to marry King Burhred of Mercia, the neighbouring kingdom; and that the prefix, "Ethel", in all the other names meant "noble" in the English tongue, but that "Alf" was the same as "elf", and meant a spirit of the earth and air.

Alfred would certainly have admitted, if he were asked, that he was proud to have been sent with this mission to Rome, in his father's name. None of his elder brothers had come.

For more detailed information, the Pope had to ask the priests and courtiers who formed the rest of the English party.

From them, he could learn that King Ethelwulf was a mild, religious man, though he could fight bravely enough when called upon. Two years before, when the Danes had stormed London and Canterbury, he had smashed them with (as the chronicler wrote) "the greatest slaughter in the heathen army that we have ever heard tell of to this present day".

The Pope must have heard their accounts of this victory with considerable pleasure. The Danes—or Northmen, or Norsemen, or Vikings, whatever you chose to call them, "white strangers" or "black strangers" or "heathen men"— had lately become the terror of Western Europe. Rome could sympathise. She had her own similar problem, the Saracens, or Moors as they were named in Spain. Their galleys swept the Mediterranean just as the Danish long-ships swept the outer ocean. Only nine years ago, these Saracens had landed near Rome herself, looting churches and defiling the very tombs of the Apostles.

Any success against the heathen, whether Dane or Saracen, came as a crumb of comfort.

How strong was King Ethelwulf? Was he the effective

overlord of all England, the "Bretwalda", as *his* father, King Egbert, had been? Or was he just the ruler of the West Saxons?

The Pope knew that England was divided into several Saxon kingdoms, and that the Welsh still held the mountainous westerly corners, Cornwall and Wales and the Lake District. The chief Saxon kingdoms were Wessex in the south, Mercia in the middle, and Northumbria in the northeast. Each in turn, starting with Northumbria, had had its age of greatness, when it had taken the lead and its kings had been looked up to as overlords by their neighbours. The turn of Wessex had come last. Alfred's grandfather had ruled Mercia as well as his own realm; he had been virtually king of all England south of the Humber.

No, the Englishman told Leo, Ethelwulf was a less ambitious man than Egbert. He was satisfied with Wessex, which meant only England south of the Thames, plus Essex to the north (but not London), and minus Cornwall in the far west. But he kept up the closest friendship with the Mercians and had given his daughter in marriage to their king.

And it was no small thing to be King of Wessex, even. The Pope would see for himself, when Ethelwulf paid his long looked-for visit to the holy city.

Leo did not live to see, but his successor did. When Alfred returned to Rome two years later, eager to point out its wonders to his father, the old gentleman who had given him the consular belt was no more. A new Pope was just elected, Benedict III, and it was to him that Ethelwulf and Alfred had to offer the splendid gifts they had brought with them. A crown of pure gold, a gold-chased sword, a gold-embroidered tunic, golden chalices for the altar, silver-gilt hanging lamps of the finest English craftsmanship, delicately woven materials . . . England was no longer an outlying, barbarous island on the fringe of the world, as she had seemed to the earlier Romans. She was among the richest and most civilised countries in Christendom.

In case any of the Roman nobility and clergy should have any doubt on this point, the new Pope advised Ethelwulf to be generous. The English king took the hint. Gold coins were distributed lavishly, and even the common people received silver. Smiles greeted the fair-skinned pilgrims wherever they went.

This time Alfred spent a whole year in Rome, and he was old enough to understand and remember much more than on his first visit. His mother, Osburh, had died a little while before they left home. Both the King and his little son were glad to forget their grief, as far as they could, among the strange sights of this far-off capital. None of the other boys had come. The eldest, in fact, was ruling Wessex on his father's behalf. Alfred had always had a rather special place in his parents' affection, as the youngest.

He was one of the few Saxon princes to have seen Rome. Almost certainly, no boy of his rank had ever spent so long there. And what a change it was, after the wandering country life at home!

For, like an old-fashioned company of strolling players, his father's court was for ever on the move. It had to be. There were no towns big enough to feed it for more than a few weeks at a time. A king had to move from one royal estate to another, using up the provisions due to him from the local farms, and then passing on. Also, to ensure that the country was properly governed and justice done, he had to supervise everything in person.

In babyhood Alfred had known the jingle of harness and the clop of hoofs as his lullaby. The sway of a wagon, or the ambling gait of a quiet horse, had rocked him as often as an indoor cradle. From the first opening of his eyes he had known the slow march of overhanging forest branches against the sky behind, and, as he had grown old enough to sit up, the view had merely changed to that of a road, stretching endlessly ahead, with the backs of jogging horsemen in the foreground. Dust and sun, mud, rain, and snow, biting winds, mist, and frost—he had known them all, as travelling companions, ever since he could remember. The two long journeys to Rome, across France and down half the length of Italy, had meant no fresh hardship, only a change of view.

It was Rome itself that was the great change. Paved streets, mighty girdling walls and towers, churches and palaces, splendid processions and services, wise and holy men reading out of books, and worldly, travelled men, with tales of far southern and eastern countries.

Even as a boy, Alfred was deeply religious. Perhaps, in those early days, there were some who thought he would become a priest. With all those elder brothers, he was not likely to be needed as a ruler. And there could not be much of an inheritance awaiting him as the youngest of the King's sons.

Yet, somehow, those who knew Alfred best could scarcely imagine him in some quiet cloister. There was another side to the boy's character. He loved tales of adventure—whether they were the old poems and stories of his Saxon forefathers or new, first-hand yarns spun by sea-captains and wandering traders. He loved all songs and music, not only the chants of the Church. And he loved sport, and looked forward to the day when he would be old enough to ride with his brothers after the red deer.

He meant to fight the Danes, too, if they came back. He had been too young to go with his father and eldest brother when they went off to beat the invaders in 851—it was even hard to be sure, now, whether he actually remembered their triumphant homecoming, or whether he only imagined he did, having heard the story so often told and re-told. He had been so very little at the time.

Would the Danes come back?

Some people said, no, they had learnt their lesson. Others said, the Danes always came back. Some said, the Danes were God's punishment for the wickedness of England. Father hoped that England had been punished enough by now, and that by coming on this pilgrimage to Rome in person, and making all these rich offerings at St. Peter's, he had earned God's forgiveness for his people. The worldlier men in Rome smiled sadly when they heard this argument. England was not the only country which suffered from these northern invaders. Nothing seemed to stop them.

They came buzzing out of Scandinavia like wasps, out of the sandy Danish creeks and the rocky Norwegian fiords. It was only partly the love of piracy which drove them. It was also sheer necessity. As the population increased, the northern countries could not support it. There was just not enough farmland. Some of the people had to move out or starve.

It was certainly true that other countries in Western Europe had suffered at least as heavily as England. In recent years Rouen, Nantes and Hamburg had been plundered, Paris and Bordeaux besieged. The dreaded long-ships had been seen as far south as Spain. They had rowed up the Guadalquivir as far as Seville—that was always their way, to use the rivers to strike at the heart of a country—but at Seville they had been beaten back by the Saracens. One scourge of Christendom had clashed with the other. It was a pity that the heathen did not meet more often to exterminate each other!

At last the long year in Rome came to an end, and the English party turned their horses' heads northwards. Ethelwulf seemed in no hurry to go home. They spent several months at the court of King Charles of the West Franks. He was the grandson of the mighty emperor, Charlemagne, and had inherited a share of his empire, the westerly French portion. There had long been a friendship between the

B

French and the English—wars between them were still far in the future—and there were old men who could remember Alfred's grandfather as a guest at Charlemagne's court, before he became King of Wessex.

King Charles had a daughter Judith. She was twelve or thirteen, twice as old as Alfred, to whom she seemed almost grown up. None the less, it came as rather a surprise when he learnt that she was going to be married to his father. He wondered how his elder brothers would feel when he brought them home a stepmother. The wedding took place at the end of the summer. It was the Archbishop of Rheims who married the middle-aged king to the girl-princess. After the usual festivities, the English party set out on the last stage of their homeward journey.

What Alfred thought of it all we do not know. But Wessex disliked the marriage exceedingly, and Ethelbald, who had been left to rule the country during his father's absence, plotted to prevent his return and to usurp the throne. Civil war was only just avoided. Ethelwulf forgave his son, and for the short remaining period of his life he shared the government with him.

Ethelwulf died when Alfred was nine. Ethelbald then became unchallenged king, and promptly caused a considerable scandal by marrying his father's widow (and his own stepmother), who was still in her 'teens. Within two years Ethelbald himself died, and his next brother, Ethelbert, became king. The interesting Judith then retired to her native country, and disappears from English history, though not entirely without trace. It is thought that Alfred may as a boy have picked up from her, or one of her Frankish attendants, the germ of the idea which grew into the Anglo-Saxon Chronicle after he became king.

One more fact about this young lady may be worth mentioning: despite the upsets caused by her first two marriages, she proceeded to shock her own family by running off with Baldwin of the Iron Arm, Count of Flanders. The iron arm seems to have been strong enough to restrain her from any further wanderings.

Meanwhile, as she sailed away from England and Alfred's next brother mounted the throne, the Danes burst into Wessex and were not driven out until they had plundered Winchester. It is scarcely surprising that, as Alfred complained in later years, his education was neglected when he was a boy.

It was as though a curse brooded over the royal family of Wessex—and in those days men really believed in curses.

One by one Ethelwulf's sons were passing away. The second, Ethelbert, reigned only five or six years. He was followed by Ethelred. Alfred was now seventeen and, though Ethelred was married and had baby sons, he was next in line to the throne until those sons should grow to manhood. In such troubled times only a grown fighting man was fit to wear a crown. Not for some centuries would it be handed on, by the strict rule of "primogeniture", to the first-born son of the previous king.

Life was uncertain, quite apart from the risks of battle. Fond though Alfred was of sport and exercise, his health was not good. Some ailment (we do not know what) dogged him through his 'teens, and another illness, more serious but equally unknown, came upon him at nineteen and afflicted him, off and on, for the rest of his life. All we know is that it brought him bouts of agonising pain, with long spells of depression between. Again, there were those who believed that he had been cursed by someone with the evil eye.

This mysterious ailment first struck him on his wedding day. For, at nineteen, he married Ealswith, a Mercian girl of royal blood.

What Ealswith looked like—or was like—is unknown. But it seems to have been a happy enough marriage, lasting all Alfred's life (she died shortly after him) and blessed with children.

What is more surprising is that we do not know what Alfred himself looked like. No statue or portrait survives, no clear description in words. If the roughly-stamped faces on his coins are meant as a likeness, they merely tell us that he was clean-shaven. The bearded figure which stands in the market-place of Wantage, his native town, is based on pure guesswork, like all other statues and pictures supposed to represent him.

There are, in fact, a great many facts about Alfred which we are never likely to know. His birthday. How, and exactly when, he died. Did he really burn the cakes when he was hiding from the Danes? And did he disguise himself as a harper and venture into their camp as a spy? We might as well clear these points out of the way at once, and admit our ignorance. They are interesting but of minor importance. In other, more vital ways, we can know Alfred more vividly than most of the public figures in today's newspaper.

That summer of his marriage to Ealswith, there was a crisis in the affairs of England.

The period of mere raids was over: the Danish invasion of England had begun in earnest.

Two or three years before, the Danes had landed in East Anglia, and, instead of sailing away again after the usual campaign in search of plunder, had moved inland and northwards into Yorkshire. There, after a tremendous battle and massacre at York itself, they had crushed the once-proud kingdom of Northumbria and destroyed it as a fighting force.

They were now firmly established in northern England. Not satisfied with this, within two years they were riding down into the Midlands, to join another army which sailed up the River Trent in long-ships. The two forces met at Nottingham, where they entrenched themselves in a great palisaded camp, with the broad stream in front and the dense oakwoods of Sherwood at their backs.

Mercia mobilised to meet the danger. Minor raids could often be dealt with by a king and his own household troops, his thanes or noblemen, and their own sworn followers. But to meet a big attack he would call out the *fyrd*, or general levy of fighting men, each armed and equipped according to his class—the poor peasant with spear and shield, the richer man with three-foot sword or battle-axe, mail shirt and helmet of iron and horn. Bows and arrows were not much used, but both spears and axes were sometimes thrown at close quarters.

Messengers were sent to King Ethelred to ask for help from Wessex. Ethelred called out his own *fyrd* and marched to join the Mercians in front of the Danish camp at Nottingham, a hundred miles north of his own borders. Alfred left his new bride, donned helmet and mail shirt, and rode with his brother.

It was his first sight of the Danes, who were to be his lifelong enemies.

There, beneath the earthen banks and stockade of the camp, lay the hated long-ships—clinker-built, oaken vessels, graceful and cruel of line, nearly eighty feet from carved beak to rudder-post. They had sixteen rowers a side and one square sail. These were the craft which had made the heathen men masters not only of every sea and coast but of every inland place that could be reached by river. "Ravens of the wind", the Danes called them, "reindeer of the breezes", and "horses of the gull's track".

And there, too, moving about on the riverside, were the heathen men themselves, with their barbaric helmets, winged or horned, and their long beards and moustaches. Their equipment was the finest in the world. Unlike the conscripted peasants of the *fyrd*, even the Danish rank-and-file were plentifully supplied with mail shirts. Their terrible battle-axes were developed from the lumber-axes they used daily in the forests at home. Their spears were strong, their swords well balanced by heavy pommels, which gave extra protection to the metal guard of the hilt.

Alfred's brother and brother-in-law, the Mercian king, had to decide whether or not to attack the camp, for the Danes showed no signs of venturing into the open. It was a hard decision. In one way it was a pity to miss the chance of a combined blow, now that the Wessex men had marched so far from their own country. But—what if the blow failed? No one had ever stormed a Danish camp successfully. Suppose the attack ended in disaster, and the Danes, sallying forth, smashed the wavering ranks of the Saxons? Then not only the north of England, but the whole of England, might be lost for ever.

The Wessex men, having come so far, favoured taking a chance. It was the Mercians, according to the later chronicler, who "made peace with the host", that is, the Danish horde. Alfred saw only a few light skirmishes before a treaty was made. Then he rode home with his people, while the Mercians collected the *geld* or ransom with which the invaders were to be bought off. Only when it was safely handed over did the Danes retire to Northumbria. They always kept their word—for the time being.

But, even back in Wessex, Alfred could not fail to be aware of the doom creeping over the island. Messengers and refugees brought the news, month by month. Bought off by Mercia, the heathen tide was flowing back over East Anglia. And by New Year, 871—Alfred's "year of battles" as it came to be called—the winged helmets were on the Thames at Reading, prepared to sweep forward into Wessex.

It was here that the chalk ridges of the Chiltern Hills faced, across the river, that other ridge of the Berkshire Downs which went slanting away into the heart of Wessex. The dry chalk, with its ancient skyline track raised high above swamp and forest, offered the perfect invasion-route for a land army.

As at Nottingham, the Danes entrenched themselves by the river. The local Saxons mustered under the elderman—or "alderman", to give the title in its modern spelling—and defeated one band of raiders, driving them back to their camp. Ethelred and his young brother were meanwhile gathering the main army of mid-Wessex. There was no time to get help from the far west. They marched on Reading with what forces they had, and the Danish outposts fell back before them. Gaining confidence, Ethelred and Alfred did what the Mercians had not dared to do at Nottingham, and swept boldly up to the Danish ramparts. They learnt, then, that perhaps the cautious Mercians had been right after all. For, as the chronicler says, "*the heathen themselves fought with valour, and rushing out of all the gates like wolves, joined battle with all their might. There for a long time both sides fought fiercely, but alas! the Christians at last turned their backs and the heathen gained the victory. . . .*"

Alfred and his brother fell back along the Berkshire Downs, rallying their forces as best they could. The war was not lost. Fresh contingents of Saxons were riding hard to join their king. The Danes made the mistake of not following up their victory. They settled down to an orgy of deep drinking, while, not twenty miles away, the Saxons recovered their strength for a counter-blow.

Ethelred did not expect the Danes to follow him at all, just at present, for he fixed his camp beneath Lowbury Hill, whereas the near-by Louse Hill (known to this day by the gipsies as "the Hill of Destruction") would have been a stronger position. So when the Danes did move out in pursuit of their enemy, after their two or three days of merry-making, they were able to occupy this higher ground themselves. They got there at dusk on 7th January, and all through that long winter night the two armies lay within a thousand yards of each other.

Dawn came. The Danes could be seen forming two

columns, one on either side of the ancient trackway. From the banners it could be seen that two Danish kings were to head one column, while their earls led the other. Ethelred held a council of war and it was decided to form two columns to meet them. He himself would attack the kings, Alfred should charge the earls. It did not occur to Ethelred that the Danes might do the attacking: it was their custom to occupy a strong position, such as a fort or some higher ground as in this case, and there await their enemies. Ethelred was so sure that the Danes would wait that he gave orders for Mass to be celebrated in his tent.

A few minutes later the Danish kings gave the word, and both the enemy columns began to pour down the slope, blowing their horns, clashing their arms, and raising a blood-curdling chorus.

Alfred and his thanes stood for a moment aghast. The Danes were now only half a mile away, coming down into the hollow between the two hills where a single thorn tree stood out as a gaunt landmark. On open ground such as this, the attacker had the advantage—the armed man, charging the last yards at full tilt, was more likely to overthrow an opponent who merely stood still and waited for him. It was not only a physical question, but a psychological one too.

There was no time to ask King Ethelred, still kneeling before the little altar set up in his tent. Alfred had to act on his own. He made a quick decision and ordered his men to charge, leading them "like a wild boar", wrote Bishop Asser, the friend who afterwards wrote his biography. Alfred's column moved forward, keeping shoulder to shoulder, locking their shields edge to edge in an overlapping "shield-wall", as far as their speed and the roughness of the ground allowed them. And Ethelred came out of his tent to see his own half of the Saxon army advancing parallel with his young brother's.

The two pairs of columns crashed, head on, in the low ground between the two hilltops. The shield-walls quivered,

were broken here and there, knit together again. The Danes
reeled from the shock and gave ground a little. Swords and
axes rose and fell in the pale January light. The hottest
struggles raged round the banners of the leaders, and amid
all stood the solitary tree, the naked thorn.

One of the two Danish kings went down. So did five of
their foremost earls, and countless numbers of their fighting
men. To this day the gipsies call that dip between the hills
"Awful Bottom", and just to the east of it they speak of "Dead
Man's Hollow".

The Danes broke and fled, back along the ridge to the
safety of their entrenchments at Reading. Alfred and his
men kept up the pursuit until nightfall. From that day the
Saxons knew—and the Danes knew too—that it was possible
for the heathen host to be beaten in fair fight.

This was the Battle of Ashdown, and it was only the first in
that year of battles. We are not sure even where they were
fought: indeed, experts argue about the site of Ashdown
itself. The results were doubtful too. In spite of the Saxon
triumph at Ashdown and their hard fighting in later engage-
ments, the end of the year found the Danes still prowling,
wolf-like, on the threshold of Wessex. But something
happened more far-reaching in its results than any of the
battles. In May, Ethelred died. His two sons were too young
to rule. Alfred became king, elected by the *witan* or council,
and "with the full consent of all the inhabitants of the
kingdom".

It was a war-worn little country he took over. By the end
of that year the fighting men of Wessex were exhausted. But
the Danes too had, for the moment, had enough. Alfred
made a treaty with them. He paid them to go away. It was
not a glorious ending to the "year of battles" which had
opened with the victory of Ashdown. But there was nothing
else to do.

At least the Danes stayed away, and the young king, still in his early twenties, had a few years of peace. Burnt homes and churches could be rebuilt, neglected land could be brought into better order, flocks and herds could be raised to their full numbers. Something perhaps could be done about the decline in education and culture which must have been developing over a long period, and which could not be blamed upon the invaders.

The monasteries, which served as the schools, the universities, and the publishing houses of those days, were no longer attracting first-class men and women in great numbers. And Wessex, which best withstood the Danes, seemed worse off in culture and education than those more northerly regions where the heathen had struck hardest. As Alfred wrote, in later years, to the Bishop of Worcester, in Mercia: "*It has often come into my remembrance what wise men there formerly were among the English race, and how foreigners came to this land for wisdom and instruction.*" But now, he went on, there was such a decline that it was the turn of the foreigners to come and teach the English. Few men could read their prayer-books even in their own language, and hardly any could translate a letter written in Latin.

Without Latin, Alfred knew, there could be no easy contact with Rome and the other courts of Christendom; no understanding of the scriptures and other books in which the wisdom of former generations was preserved.

Education, however, was a slow process. Dear though it was to his heart, there was not much he could do in the first years of his reign.

Meanwhile he grappled with the day-to-day problems of governing, and enjoyed a happy family-life with Ealswith. Children came: first a girl, Ethelflaed, then a boy, Edward, destined to carry on the royal line. In all, Alfred was to have three sons, of whom one died young, and three daughters.

The Danes busied themselves elsewhere. They always

followed the line of least resistance. They had turned to England, of late, because on the whole it now offered more loot and less organised resistance than either Ireland, France or Spain. And in England they were leaving Wessex, the toughest foe, until the end. Northumbria they had smashed at York; East Anglia was too small a region to offer much resistance; Mercia, weak-spirited, had become a "collaborator" —Alfred's brother-in-law, King Burhred, retired to Rome and the Danes set up a Saxon puppet ruler to act under their orders.

The Danes were nearly ready to take their last bite.

Alfred had been king for about four years when the heathen wolf-pack snapped again at Wessex—but failed to get their teeth into a vital spot.

The Danes broke through to Wareham, in Dorset, and then to Exeter, further along the south coast. Alfred fought them on land and sea. The war lasted a year or two in all, and was ended by a stroke of luck. The Danish fleet was wrecked off the Dorset coast, near Swanage. One hundred and twenty long-ships were destroyed in the storm, with untold casualties. Each vessel held about fifty men. Some of the six thousand, despite the weight of mail-shirts and armlets, may have struggled ashore or been picked up by their comrades. At all events, the disaster was so great that the Danes hurriedly made peace, offered Alfred as many hostages as he liked, and withdrew their army into Mercia.

It was a merry Christmas, that year, in Wessex. More than for many long years past it must have been a season of hope. Church and cathedral echoed with exultant music as the Saxons celebrated the birth of the child Christ and the assurance of God's love for men which it implied. Was not the storm at Swanage a proof that God would deliver the Christian from the heathen? And when High Mass gave place to feasting in the hall, and feasting in turn gave place to singing and story-telling, what a moment to recall old times

and bygone victories, to shake the oaken rafters with
thunderous laughter and song!

Christmas was a leisurely festival, extending over twelve
days—for what were twelve days, when the daylight was at its
shortest, the land probably too frozen or too flooded for
work, and the stock reduced to a minimum, because of the
shortage of winter feed? Christmas was a time to rest, relax,
and rejoice, and to dream of spring.

The Danes waited until the end of the festival period,
Twelfth Night, and then they struck.

Their leader was a king named Guthrum, who had led the
invasion into Dorset a year or two before. The losses at
Swanage had been made good, for the Danes were continually getting reinforcements, either from home or from
their other armies. They had a loose but convenient organisation. Groups were banded together under leaders, with an
arrangement to share their plunder; these groups in turn
combined to form armies, perhaps only for a single campaign.
And there might be a much looser kind of co-operation
between armies and fleets a great distance apart.

Guthrum, for instance, seems to have had an understanding
with another Danish commander, whose host spent that
winter in South Wales. Suppose these other Danes crossed
the Bristol Channel and landed in North Devon? Suppose the
"Welshmen" of Cornwall, who had no love for the Saxons,
could be used as allies to make trouble in the far west? And
suppose Guthrum himself, then at Gloucester, made a surprise
thrust into Wiltshire and down into Hampshire? The long
narrow kingdom of Wessex would be cut through the middle
from Thames to English Channel. The western half, still rich
and most of it never before touched by Danish raids, would
be crushed between Guthrum and his allies in Devon and
Cornwall. The easterly half could be rolled up at leisure,
later on.

It was a masterly plan, and it began with a master-stroke.

Guthrum gathered his men, made a surprise march, and pounced on Chippenham, a little town beside the Wiltshire Avon. It is not certain whether Alfred was there at the time. Usually the royal family spent Christmas at Dorchester, but one of the King's estates *was* at Chippenham, and it had been the place chosen, long ago, for the marriage of his sister to the Mercian king. So it might well have been honoured with Alfred's presence for the festival.

Wherever Alfred was, he was taken off his guard. There was no time to call out the *fyrd*. With his thanes and household troops he fell back into the woods and swamps of Somerset. Not—as the old stories suggest—as a desperate fugitive, alone and helpless. He had men with him and all the resources of West Somerset and Devon to back him. The swamps, which were later to be known as Sedgemoor and give their name to another historic campaign, guarded the gap between two walls of hills, the Quantocks and the Blackdowns. Lurking with a small force there, Alfred could bar Guthrum's path if he chose to move westwards towards that gap. If Guthrum moved south towards Winchester and the English Channel, Alfred was still a threat to his flank.

Guthrum must have known this. Though his raiders thrust on into Hampshire, spreading panic there and driving the more frightened inhabitants overseas, he himself spent the rest of the winter round Chippenham.

He realised that there was still Alfred to be dealt with.

Sedgemoor is really sedge-mere—not a moor at all, that is, but a vast expanse of flat land, in those days continually flooded by its rivers or the near-by sea. Only in modern times have embankments and drains turned it into farmland. Its homesteads and hamlets still stand, as they have stood for centuries, on the knobs and patches of higher ground, which every few years, when there are especially bad floods, become again the islets they were in Alfred's day. It is easier then to imagine the scene as it once was. One has only to blot out, in the mind's eye, the fences and telegraph-poles and other modern objects which stand out of the leaden water, substitute reeds, and clothe the higher ground with trees and undergrowth. The horizon is unchanged—eastwards the grey wall of the Mendips, southwards the Blackdowns, westwards the gracefully dipping wave of the Quantocks. Unchanged too are the island silhouettes—the long, low outline of the tiny Polden range, the shark-fin of Glastonbury Tor, King Arthur's Avalon. And, while thinking of Alfred, it is hard not to remember Arthur too. Surely Tennyson had this landscape in mind when he wrote *Morte d'Arthur?*

> *"On one side lay the Ocean, and on one*
> *Lay a great water, and the moon was full."*

And:

> *"I heard the water lapping on the crag,*
> *And the long ripple washing in the reeds."*

Into these fenland fastnesses Alfred and his small force retreated to gather their strength again. Life was rough, but they were neither friendless nor starving. Some of the near-by villages were royal manors; any of the others would, in such an emergency, spare the King what they could from their limited winter stores. But it *was* winter, in one of the dampest, coldest spots imaginable, and they were fighting a guerrilla campaign. Probably no other English king has ever lived so hard, at least within his own realm.

It was only for a few months, however, not for several years as the old stories relate.

Through January, February, and most of March, Alfred was continually on the move. Then about Easter, which fell that year on 23rd March, there came great news from the west: the thanes of Devon had smashed the other Danish army which had invaded them from South Wales. The Danish king was dead, his famous Raven banner captured, his force almost annihilated. And with those Danes died any hope of stirring up the Cornishmen to stab the Saxons in the back. The pincer movement had failed: Alfred had only the one enemy, Guthrum, to deal with.

This was the moment when he established his famous fort on the island of Athelney and intensified his raids against the Danes.

Athelney covered a mere twenty-four acres of ground, raised thirty or forty feet above the general level of the fens. Writing three hundred years later, when it could not have changed much, William of Malmesbury, a monkish historian and himself a Somerset man, wrote that it was *"not an island of the sea, but so cut off by flooded marshes and bogs that it can only be reached by boat"*. Athelney was densely clothed with alders, giving shelter to deer and other game.

Huts were built and no doubt a stockade, but Alfred had no intention of staying there for long. Messengers were sent out. The scattered fighting men of Wiltshire and Hampshire were bidden to prepare for the great day. The King was coming back to them, out of the west, bringing with him the fresh and untouched levies of Somerset. They were to meet at Egbert's Stone, a landmark on high ground at the junction of the three shires. The place lay in Selwood, one of the vast English forests which has long been only a dim memory.

The day fixed was in mid-May, about Whitsuntide. For hours the different bands came trooping in, some mounted, some on foot, their newly-burnished arms twinkling in the sunlight which filtered through the young leaves. Alfred rode in from Athelney, and the oaken aisles of the forest must have echoed with their welcome, for they saw him *"as one restored to life after many tribulations"*.

It was a short campaign. One day's march, one more night in camp, and then battle.

The fight took place at Ethandun, probably the modern Edington, on the chalk downs of Wiltshire. Guthrum's whole army was mustered, and the struggle was fierce and long. But Alfred's advancing shield-wall held firm. At last the Danes turned and fled for the safety of their camp at Chippenham. The Saxons remounted—for even the horsemen fought on foot—and galloped on their heels, cutting down all the fugitives they could.

For two weeks Alfred besieged Guthrum at Chippenham. Then the Danes surrendered, a treaty was made, and after three weeks Guthrum was baptised a Christian. Alfred himself stood godfather to his enemy.

The great victory of Ethandun was not, unfortunately, the end of Alfred's struggle with the Danes.

Even Guthrum was to break his word and slip back into his old ways until, after a second sharp lesson, he settled down under his new Christian name, Athelstan, as King of East Anglia. Nor were other Danish adventurers bound by Guthrum's promises. To the very end of his life Alfred had still to reckon with Danish invasions, as did his son and grandson after him, but the dark days of Athelney were never to return.

Alfred's agreement with Guthrum left the Danes holding the eastern counties, but their puppet ruler disappeared from Mercia and that one-time independent kingdom came under the overlordship of Wessex again. Alfred's eldest daughter married the elderman, Ethelred, and herself bore the title, Lady of the Mercians, but there was no question but that Alfred was now King of all England, outside the Danish occupied territory. His second daughter in due time became Abbess of Shaftesbury, and the youngest, Alfthryth, married Baldwin II, Count of Flanders, son of the romantic Judith who had once run away with "Iron Arm".

Alfred's first concern was to strengthen the defence of his

ALFRED THE GREAT

enlarged kingdom. Long ago, in Spain, the Saracens had
shown that ships were the best safeguard against pirates.
Alfred took note. He had already gone to sea against his
enemies, and now he became the founder of the first regular
English navy. Progress was gradual, but towards the end of
his reign he commissioned new and bigger warships to his
own designs, twice as long as the Danish vessels, carrying
sixty oars to their thirty. He brought shipbuilders over from
Frisia (now part of Holland) and stiffened his navy with
volunteers from the same country.

But raiders might always slip through defences in that age
of oars and clumsy sails and lack of radio-communication.
So Alfred established fortified towns or "boroughs" to hold
his frontiers and coasts, and to command key-points on the
rivers up which the enemy might sail. The labour and expense
caused a good deal of murmuring among the people, for not
every Saxon had learnt from the Danes, as the King had, what
a vital part such strong-points could play. Altogether, Alfred
founded or re-founded about twenty-five towns.

One other lesson he had absorbed: the Dane, as a full-time
professional fighter, had always the advantage over the Saxon
conscript, who had half his mind on the neglected fields at
home. Alfred could not afford a big standing army but he
lightened the burden as much as he could. The *fyrd* was
divided into two groups, only one of which was liable to duty
at a given time.

Having cleared his realm of enemies and barred the door
against them, Alfred was able at last to set his house in order.

The turmoil of the Danish wars—the burning of property
and records, the ebb and flow of refugees, the looting and
general scattering of possessions—had spread confusion
everywhere, tempting and assisting thieves and criminals of
all types. The general decay of religion added to the
immorality and lawlessness.

Alfred set out to restore law and order. He could not

point to a row of printed volumes: unwritten custom was a big element in Saxon behaviour, there were no Acts of Parliament, and custom varied locally. Alfred is remembered as "the law-giver", but he did not dictate a whole code of new rules of his own. More tactfully, he had the old laws collected, written down, and published, even though in some cases, dating from different times and districts, they might seem to contradict one another. The main thing was that people in future had something in black and white to guide them. If they interpreted these in the light of Christianity and local custom, they would not go far wrong.

"In the light of Christianity . . ." Alfred knew that mere laws and punishments would not ensure a decent national life, yet the Church could be of little use until its standards were raised, especially its standards of scholarship.

He summoned to his court all the men of learning he could attract. It is clear that Wessex had fallen to a low level, educationally, because most of these scholars came from other regions.

Asser, who came unwillingly at first but remained as a staunch admirer of Alfred and wrote his biography, was a Welshman. There were several Mercians, Grimbald from France, John the Old Saxon (that is, from the original Saxon homeland in Germany), John the Scot, and others.

Feeling that the wisdom and knowledge of the past were enshrined in Latin, the common language of all Christian scholars, Alfred lamented the decline of Latin in his own kingdom. But, while doing all he could to restore it, he was determined to open the doors of learning to a wider public. He wished to see *"all the freeborn youth of England set to learning until they can well read English writing"*. He founded a school at court where the youngest of his own sons studied with other children of noble birth, so that in later years England had what no other western country possessed, a ruling class of laymen who could read. He stimulated learning everywhere.

It is reckoned that nearly half his revenue was spent, in one way or another, on educational purposes. One feels sad that one cannot believe the legend that he founded University College, Oxford—though it seems true enough that he founded Oxford as a town.

Alfred was not content to wait until the next generation grew up to take over the government. He tackled their fathers on the spot. Aldermen and other officials were given strong hints that they had better learn to read if they hoped to continue in positions of responsibility. Old men went to their lessons. Alfred set the example. He was never too proud to learn. Though he could read and write his own language, he found Latin as stiff an obstacle as any modern schoolboy has ever done. But he ground away at it as doggedly as he had fought the Danes.

Latin, he realised, was not for everybody. The rest must be satisfied with reading English—but what *was* there for them to read? So he embarked on another ambitious task, the translation into English of the best Latin books he knew.

He chose parts of the Bible, and books on theology, philosophy, history and geography, by such men as Bede and Boethius, Orosius and Gregory. Where necessary, he adapted and modernised the text to make it clear to English readers. Much of what we know about his character is deduced from these personal touches. He did a great deal of the translation himself, but he had help from Asser, from Werferth, Bishop of Worcester, and from other friends.

Once, when he was talking to Asser, he was struck by a certain passage in a book they were discussing. Pulling out a little prayer-book from the folds of his tunic, he asked Asser to copy the quotation into the margin. Asser could not find enough room, so he took a clean quire of parchment, saying that there might be other extracts to copy down later. There were. In time the eight leaves of the original quire grew into a whole volume of quotations—*flosculos*, or "little flowers", culled from the Gospels or whatever Alfred happened to be reading. They called the book by the Greek name of *Encheiridion*, that is a "handbook" or "manual", and Alfred kept it by him night and day.

One of Alfred's greatest literary works was his foundation of the *Anglo-Saxon Chronicle*, a national record instead of a mere local one such as various monasteries had kept before. It is thought that he took the idea from the West Franks. It is a history of varying quality and value (the early parts, dealing with events outside living memory, are naturally less reliable), but it was continued right into the twelfth century. Alfred either wrote or supervised the part compiled in his own lifetime, but it was never used, as it would have been by most monarchs, to glorify his own actions.

Truth-teller, law-giver, England's darling, shepherd of the English—these are some of the descriptions given to Alfred by those who knew him, or who came soon after him. It was not until the seventeenth century that any writer spoke of him as "the Great".

One quality which must have struck his friends was his self-discipline. Racked by pain, haunted by depression, beset by public cares, Alfred never gave in. There was so much to do, so much to learn. Having no clock, he measured his days by candles, inventing a horn lantern to make sure they burned evenly. Not a minute was wasted. He would deliver judgment in a law case while he washed his hands. There must be time for reading and translation, time for exercise, for talk with learned friends or with sea-captains who had sailed the Polar seas, time for a warm and affectionate family-life, time to invest his little grandson Athelstan, at an unusually early age, with the scarlet cloak, jewelled belt, and sword in a golden scabbard, which betokened a royal thane.

Alfred died in his early fifties. *"So long as I have lived,"* he had written, *"I have striven to live worthily. I desire to leave the men who come after me a remembrance in good works."* There was

no doubt he had succeeded. He had left his people a legacy
which cannot be measured.

One day, in that darkest of his winters, he lost an ornament,
a small jewel, not far from Athelney. It was found more than
eight hundred years later, and today it lies in the Ashmolean
Museum at Oxford. It is a fine example of Anglo-Saxon art,
carried out in gold, enamel, and rock crystal. It shows a tiny
figure, and round the curved edge run these words:

AELFRED MEC HEHT GEWYRCAN.

"*Alfred had me made* . . ."

Not only the little jewel, but England herself, might have
said that.

THE YEARS BETWEEN 901–1026

In the century and a quarter between the death of Alfred and the birth of William the Conqueror ordinary life in England did not change greatly. Wars continued. The Danes could never be dislodged from the eastern counties of the "Danelaw", but, on the other hand, they never managed to conquer the rest of the country. Gradually Saxon and Dane learnt to live as neighbours, and soon, by intermarriage, as kinsmen. They were not so far removed in stock and language that they could not develop a sense of unity. There was one moment, just before William the Conqueror was born, when it looked as though this newly-mixed nation might become just one dominion of a Scandinavian empire. That was in 1018, when Canute, besides being accepted as King of England, was also ruler of Norway and Denmark. But the moment passed. Canute's sons could not hold their inheritance together, and the Godwins of Wessex brought back the old Saxon royal line in Edward the Confessor. England remained an island apart, firmly English.

Men ploughed their fields as they had done in Alfred's time. The towns might be a little bigger, but not much. Little monasteries and nunneries kept the light of religion and scholarship alive, but the whole tempo was slow and easy. "Progress", as an idea, was unknown. Many people believed that the world would end with the millennium, or first thousand years after Christ. But the sacred anniversary came and went without incident, and life jogged on in the green, half-empty island of fields and forests, criss-crossed with the fading tracks of ancient Rome.

2

William: The Self-Made King

ON a steep hill above the small town of Falaise in Normandy
there still stands the castle, its keep massive and square above
the billowing softness of the tree-tops. And until 1944,
certainly, the tannery still remained where it had always been,
its sheds and yard grouped on the banks of the stream at the
foot of the hill. But in that summer, when the allied forces
landed in Normandy to liberate Europe from Hitler, the
horrors of modern warfare exploded in Falaise. Nine-tenths
of the town was destroyed. Only the castle clung, eagle-
proud, to its rocky perch, scarred and shaken but still itself.
The core of that castle is more than nine hundred years old,
the later parts are newer by a mere century or so. It is still
true to say, then, that *"this* was the castle".

Here, in the year 1026, lived the young bachelor Count of
Hiesmois, brother to the Duke of Normandy. To his face
the Count was referred to as "Robert the Magnificent":
behind his back, he was more commonly nicknamed "Robert
the Devil". And a magnificent young devil he probably was
—strong-willed, passionate, swaggering, and on occasion
(like all his folk) cruel. For the Dukes of Normandy, though
they had been frenchified for a century, were sprung from
Viking stock. Their ancestor was that Rolf or Rollo who
had brought his long-ships up the Seine, and, proving too
tough to turn out, had been accepted as the duke of that
region. "Northman" had become "Norman", pagan had
become Christian, but some of the Viking blood still ran in

their veins, though even the words on their lips had changed to French.

That was Robert, then, living in the grim square tower on the rock.

At the bottom of the hill lived Fulbert the tanner. And Fulbert had a daughter, Arletta. And Arletta had attractions which Robert did not fail to notice as he rode up and down, past the tannery, between his castle and the town.

A tanner's daughter was hardly suitable for a countess, but Robert fell deeply in love with her. If he could not marry Arletta, he would certainly marry no one else. Nobody could dictate to Robert the Devil.

So it was that, in the following year, 1027, a child was born to Arletta in a small dark room in the castle—little more than a windowless recess, carved out of the wall of the keep which there is five yards thick. They called him William. History was to add, "the Conqueror".

A few months later, Robert's elder brother died suddenly. There were those who said that Robert had helped him out of the world with poison. At all events Robert was not sorry to become Duke of Normandy in his place.

William—soon to be joined by a baby sister, Adelaide— was a good-looking little boy with dark hair and grey eyes. He showed personality and strength of will from early years. People used to say, afterwards, that even as a new-born child he showed his character by the way he clutched the rushes on the floor of that dark little room where he lay. As a five-year-old he was the natural leader of his gang of young friends, drilling and dominating them all.

The typical education of a Norman boy is summed up in what another duke had said, a generation or two before. "My son must be noble among nobles, scholarly among scholars, steady in the saddle, swift in the field. He must know all the lore of the countryside, the bends of the rivers, the boundaries of meadow and woodland. He must know how to fly his falcon, cast a net, throw a javelin, slip a hound, and slay a deer." This, in general, was the course William followed, as his later life shows, except that opinions differ about his book-learning. Certainly his father was in no position to lecture him on that point. He himself, when a boy, was said to have stabbed the tutor who rebuked him for idleness. After that he had taken to the forest for a time, with a band of rascally followers. He was well-named Robert the Devil.

There is an old saying, when the Devil is sick, the Devil a saint would be, and, when William was seven, his father showed the truth of it. He announced he was going on pilgrimage to the Holy Land. He was not well, and he might never return. In that case, William was to have the dukedom.

When he announced this to his assembled barons, there was a murmur of objection. William was too young. William found himself lifted in his father's brawny arms, heard his father laugh and cry: "He is only little, yes, my lords, but he will grow." Pushed to it, the barons came out with their other objection: William was basely born, his mother no rightful duchess but only the tanner's daughter of Falaise. The Duke retorted that William was the only son he had or was likely to have. The barons had to accept his decision. The dukedom was, after all, Robert's to give away as he liked. The Normans had none of that idea which the Saxons held across the Channel—the first faint gleam of democracy —that a ruler must be accepted and approved by his people.

The barons knelt and swore allegiance to the boy, and Duke Robert departed on his journey.

For a long time news of him was scarce and doubtful. A pilgrim named Pirou turned up with the report that he had met the Duke at the gates of Jerusalem. The Duke had not been well, for he was lying in a litter, carried by four swarthy natives. But he had managed, with a flash of his old spirit, to joke about the situation. "You can say," he told Pirou, "that you met me being borne off to Paradise by four black devils!" Silence and rumours followed. At last it was confirmed that Robert had died on the way home. William was Duke of Normandy.

What did that mean? Though he had barons and bishops to act for him until he was older, William already had a fair notion of what it meant to be Duke of Normandy.

It meant that in a few years' time, when he was free of his guardians, he would be absolute lord of this little country. For, though the King of France was rather vaguely thought of as an overlord, the Norman dukes took practically no notice of him.

Normandy was a little world of its own. It lay along the coast, its pale chalk cliffs looking across the Channel to the very similar English cliffs just beyond the horizon. To the east was Flanders, to the west Brittany, with their own separate rulers, and inland, up the Seine, were the King's own territories.

A green land, Normandy, a land of woods and fields and orchards. There were towns—Rouen, Caen, Bayeux, Falaise, Harfleur—and a thick sprinkling of castles, his own and his barons'. For it was the Norman way to fight from castles or, if caught in the open, to fight on horseback with the lance. The Saxons, William learnt, were quite different in their methods: they troubled less with castles and fought from choice in the open, having reached the battlefield, they preferred to dismount and fight it out with sword and axe.

Fighting was important. It was certain to play a big part in his life. William must have realised that from his earliest years. If we are to understand William—or any other nobleman of the medieval period—we must get the reasons for this quite clear in our own minds.

Otherwise the Middle Ages will remain (as they have done to millions of puzzled school-children) a meaningless muddle of sieges, rebellions, plots, raids, and family-feuds. Why *did* barons fight so much? These galloping men in mail, who form so large a part of the pageant of medieval history, did not gallop solely for exercise.

When William could say to himself, "Normandy is mine, now," he meant it literally. The land was his. As he could not look after it all himself, much of it was held by lesser lords or by monasteries, who paid him contributions in return. Cash played a small part in everyday life and few coins were circulated, so the Duke's income came in to him in various forms. It might be corn or eggs or fish or any other foodstuff, cloth or timber or hay, falcons or horses or hounds. Much of it would be in service—military service or labour of one sort and another.

The bigger a lord's territory, the bigger his income. Hence wars between duchies and nations.

The weaker a lord's authority, the more chance for his underlings, or vassals, to avoid paying him what they were supposed to. Hence armed rebellion and defiance, when the vassal thought he could get away with it.

The bigger the number of a lord's sons, the smaller the share of lands for each. Hence family-feuds, and civil war even between brother and brother, or father and son.

True, many noblemen liked fighting for its own sake and bracketed it in their minds with hunting and other exciting sports. True, they were trained for it, and, unless they became priests, no other profession was open to them. But the taste and the training did not *cause* the warfare, they developed because of the way in which the medieval world was organised.

If we are still puzzled that these knights and barons should be willing to risk death and injury, mainly to extract a larger income from their lands or to withhold due payment from their overlords, we should turn for a moment and glance at our own age. Here we see plenty of people, some perfectly honest and some less so, risking bankruptcy to make more money, and not a few dishonest ones risking prison to cheat the tax-collector.

Under their mail-shirts the Norman blood—under their cone-shaped helmets the Norman head—worked very much the same.

That was what the Duke of Normandy had to reckon with. And it was not easy, when you were only eight or nine.

William's mother married, now, a knight named Sir Herluin de Conteville—it was hardly safe for a woman to remain single, unless she became a nun, and certainly Arletta, the despised daughter of the tanner, who had cast her spell on Duke Robert, had more than her share of enemies. She, more than most, needed the protection of a husband.

William had his guardians, appointed by his father. Anyhow, a boy of his age spent more time with the men than with any mother. But the link of family affection was strong, and when Sir Herluin and Arletta had children he proved a staunch half-brother to them. There were two boys and a girl in Arletta's second family. The elder boy, Odo, was later Bishop of Bayeux and William's life-long helper. The younger boy was christened Robert, which was a trifle tactless on Arletta's part.

When not touring his duchy, William kept his court in Rouen, the cathedral-city near the mouth of the Seine. Here, until he was entering his 'teens, he had the company of his older cousin Edward, the exiled heir to the English throne, then held by Danish usurpers. This was the gentle, religious Edward who earned the nickname of "the Confessor". Growing up in Normandy, Edward picked up a preference for French ways and a healthy respect for his masterful young cousin. These facts were to be important in the future history of England and Normandy.

William was about fourteen when Edward left Rouen to become King of England, largely through the influence of the leading English earl, Godwin of Wessex. It was this Godwin's son, Harold, who was later to fight William at Hastings. So, one by one, the chief characters in the drama take the stage: Edward the Confessor, William, and Harold. Edward married Harold's sister, Edith. There was thus a family-link between them all.

William was a far-sighted person, given to long brooding silences, and—though he could also fly into a rage—extremely patient. But even William could not possibly see, at this period, that twenty-four years after Edward's crowning he would be a claimant to that crown himself.

It was all he could do to manage Normandy. A boy-duke was a temptation to many barons to avoid paying their dues. There were plots and revolts. His three guardians were murdered. William called together the chief men in Normandy and took another guardian on their advice. Actually this man, Ralph of Wacey, was one of the murderers, but there is an old principle that an ex-poacher makes the best gamekeeper, and in this case it was sound. Ralph did not betray him. But with such a guardian William had to walk warily. So, even in boyhood, he learnt to tread the tight-rope of danger.

The worst peril came when he was twenty and had taken up his full powers as Duke.

He was hunting—it was a life-long passion of his—and a plot was made to surprise him at his lodge in the forest, at Valognes. His cousin Guy of Burgundy led the conspiracy. William was to be killed or made captive.

William had the narrowest of escapes. He rode headlong eastwards to Falaise, where he knew he could rely on the loyalty of his native town. But he could not muster enough troops of his own to deal with Guy, so he rode away to Poissy, where King Henry of France received him and promised military aid. Then followed William's famous first battle at Val-ès-dunes, just east of Caen, about which

Hilaire Belloc wrote a splendid (but as he said himself "grossly unhistorical") poem:

"And now, go forward, Normandy,
    Go forward all in one.
The press was caught and trampled and it broke
From the sword and its swinger and the axe's stroke,
Pouring through the gap in a whirl of smoke
    As a blinded herd will run.
And so fled many and a very few
With mounts all spent would staggering pursue,
But the race fell scattered as the evening grew;
    The battle was over and done.

> *Like birds against the reddening day*
>   *They dwindled one by one,*
> *And I heard a trumpet far away*
>   *At the setting of the sun."*

As Belloc himself points out, it was not so much William who won the victory as the troops lent him by the King. But a great victory it was, and from that day William was able to win his own battles.

He was a man now, tall, good-looking, with high temples, a keen glance in his grey eyes, and strong, stern features, which could sometimes soften into a smile of great charm. So far he had shown little interest in girls, but about this time he made up his mind that he would marry Matilda, the daughter of his neighbour, the Count of Flanders.

Matilda had other views. She was a beautiful girl, then about seventeen, proud of her noble ancestry (which included Alfred the Great of England), and a lover of poetry and art. She had a mind of her own. Already she herself had suggested marrying an English aristocrat. He had snubbed her, and she was in the worst possible mood when her parents told her of

William's proposal. Never, she retorted, would she wed the low-born grandson of the Falaise tanner.

Her remarks (and even the most refined young ladies were apt to be outspoken in that century) were all too accurately reported to William. An insult to his parentage was something he could not bear. Once, when besieging some rebels in Alençon, he was mocked by skins hung from the battlements and the jeering cry of "Hides for the tanner!" He took a terrible revenge on the men responsible.

How, though, to deal with Matilda of Flanders? The young man did not hesitate. He took horse and galloped over the frontier to her father's palace at Lille. He burst into the room where she was, before anyone could announce him, seized her by her long plaits, knocked her about for some moments, hurled her to the floor, and then departed as he had come, without formality.

Matilda found this passionate young man irresistible in more senses than one. She raised no further objection to the marriage. But the Church did, for there was a faint degree of relationship between the two families, and this time the authorities chose to be awkward.

William found himself up against his latest friend and adviser, a remarkable Italian monk named Lanfranc, who was destined to be one of the greatest influences in William's life. Lanfranc was more than twenty years older than he; a man of high birth and even higher intellect; a Greek scholar in an age when Greek was almost forgotten in Western Europe; a Churchman, an educationist, an organiser, and a lawyer. He was then Prior of Bec, which he had entered because it was "the poorest monastery he could find", but which he made a renowned centre of learning. When the Pope banned the proposed marriage, Lanfranc supported the Pope. William flew into another of his rages and looted the monastery lands at Bec. He banished Lanfranc from his duchy, but the Prior behaved with such dignity and courage that the quarrel was later made up between them. After four years, William and Matilda ignored the ban and got married.

In the year before their wedding, William paid his first visit to England, to see his cousin King Edward, whom he had known so well in boyhood. There was always a good deal of contact between the two countries, for Edward admired everything Norman and gave great offence to many of his subjects by giving high positions to men from across the Channel. The Bishop of London was a Norman. So were some of the King's chaplains.

Normans were often surprised by the wealth and civilisation of Edward's England. In size, of course, it was many times larger than their own country. It was well farmed and, as the climate was probably milder than it is now, there were vineyards in the southern districts. There were many towns and sea-ports, and a busy traffic with the outside world. The arts and crafts reached a high standard. Matilda, later on, was to be particularly proud of a dress made for her by one of her English ladies-in-waiting, and to mention it specially in her will. English coins were particularly beautiful in Edward's reign; after the Norman Conquest they were cruder, and it was a hundred years or more before the mints got back to their old quality of design. Despite Danish havoc, the monasteries were full of precious articles.

William's keen grey eyes took in the scene and his hard head was busy. What was to happen to this country when his gentle cousin died? Edward had no son. The next heir —near in blood but far in space—lived in Hungary and was a mere name to the English. Of course, the Danes would probably try to move in and make a final effort to bring the island into the family-circle of Scandinavia. Against them, the jumped-up Godwin, Earl of Wessex, and Edward's father-in-law, might try to take the throne for his family.

The future was quite uncertain. No one could tell how long Edward would live. In fact, he lived nearly fourteen years after that visit of William's, whereas the powerful Godwin died quite soon afterwards. Harold took over his father's estates. Harold, now, would be the man to reckon with.

Years passed. William and Matilda had children, both boys and girls. William strengthened his control of Normandy and enlarged his power by taking over the smaller territory of Maine to the south. He won the title of "Conqueror" long before he sailed against England. For all he knew, his future might lie entirely on the Continent. He was brave, but no gambler.

He had luck which any gambler might have envied. In 1064 Harold was sailing in the Channel and was wrecked on the French coast. He was seized by the local lord, Guy of Ponthieu, with a view to ransom. William heard and wasted no time. Before Harold could be ransomed, he virtually "bought" him from Guy. It was all done under a cover of friendliness. Harold was received as an honoured guest at the Norman court, but he knew that he had only exchanged one prison for another.

Men argued afterwards—and have argued ever since—just what William and Harold agreed together.

The Normans said that Harold did homage to William and became "his man", and that he promised William the crown of England when Edward died.

The English said that neither Harold nor even Edward himself could promise William any such thing, because only the Council could choose a new sovereign. Kingship in England was an office to which a man was elected, not a private possession to be handed on. Anyhow, promises made under threats were not real promises at all, and if (as some said) William had tricked Harold into swearing over a hidden collection of holy relics, no such oath was binding. As for the "homage", it depended what was meant by the ceremony. Harold had understood it simply as a formal expression of thanks to William for saving him from Guy of Ponthieu.

Both William and Harold were largely sincere in the views they held. The tragedy of Hastings, two years later, was not the clash of hero and villain (from whichever side it is looked at) but the conflict of two brave men, each having a great deal of justification for what he did.

So Harold went back to England, where his presence was soon badly needed to deal with rebellion in the north, which the King could not have coped with. And within a year or so Edward fell ill during the Christmas festival, and died in the first week of the New Year.

It was the fateful year of 1066.

The news crossed the sea to Normandy and William swore one of his passionate oaths.

Harold had played him false! The dying King had recommended Harold as his successor, the Council had accepted his recommendation—and Harold had accepted the crown. Not a day had been lost. The mourners had turned from the grave to escort Harold to his throne. The coronation had been held in the newly-built abbey of Westminster which had been Edward's dearest project.

A lesser man than William would have raged vainly, and then admitted himself beaten.

What, after all, could he do? Harold had been practical ruler of England, in Edward's name, for some time past. Now he openly wore the crown. It was the depth of winter. He had months in which to strengthen himself before any enemy could cross the sea to challenge him.

And what then? How could little Normandy challenge England? There were good English ships to meet in the Channel before even a landing could be made. Those passed, there were the swarming soldiers of England—those stalwart, dogged fellows, bigger on the average than Normans, wielding frightful Danish axes that would go through chain-mail as though it were linen. And at their head would be Harold, the now-familiar figure whose abilities William had learnt to respect—Harold, with his blue eyes and drooping fair moustache, Harold the brave soldier and the skilful general, under his gold-wrought standard, the Standard of the Fighting Man.

The odds seemed hopelessly balanced against success. William brooded over the problem. Were the odds as heavy as they seemed? And could the balance be altered in his favour?

The English were strong, yes. United, they could hardly be beaten. But *were* they united? Harold was not of the old royal house. He had his enemies. There were men in England who thought themselves as good as Harold. Such men would not fight for William against him, but they might hang back and not help Harold, thinking that Harold and William would cancel each other out, leaving themselves in power.

So, thought William, England might be weaker than she seemed. Was Normandy stronger than she seemed? Or could she be made so?

Normandy could not be more united than she was. Long ago, he had seen to that. Her man-power was solid behind him, but it was just not big enough to take over England. He must have more troops. Not allies—allies meant other dukes or kings in equal partnership, and he wanted no partners. Volunteers! That was the solution. Individuals and small bands, enlisting under his banner, all bound by allegiance to him. . . .

William began a skilful propaganda campaign throughout Europe. It was his view of the dispute that was spread and accepted everywhere—all the more easily because it fitted in with the general practice on the Continent. Crowns *were* regarded as personal property, to be left by one king to another. William's case was that Edward had promised the crown to him, and that Harold had sworn to help him. Edward's death-bed recommendation of Harold was easy to explain away. Harold's conduct was not. In Europe few people understood the English viewpoint, that neither Edward nor Harold had been free to promise anything, and that only the English could appoint an English king.

William sent his friend Lanfranc to Rome, to see the Pope. The shrewd Italian put William's case with his usual brilliance. The Pope did not hear Harold's side at all. He decided in favour of William and blessed his enterprise, thus turning it into something like a crusade.

Volunteers began to pour in. The Pope's blessing made the expedition respectable: the promise of land and loot made it attractive. From Flanders and Brittany, from Aquitaine and Provence, from beyond the Alps, even, in Italy, knights were strung along the roads which led to Normandy. They were "soldiers of fortune" in the truest sense. William smiled as the numbers mounted. With luck, everything was going to be all right.

That summer he had the devil's own luck.

He was ready to sail by mid-August, but the wind was against him and he could not set out until the end of September. That delay, however maddening it was at the time, was his salvation.

The simple problem of food and forage made it hard to keep a big army together for long. William managed it by good organisation, so that his army held out in Normandy without either starving or looting the countryside. The English *fyrd*, mustered to meet William on the Sussex beaches, stayed as long as they could, and then were forced to disband.

So, too, with Harold's ships patrolling the Channel. They could not keep at sea for ever. They had to pass through the Dover Straits and sail round to the Thames for stores and refitting—just before the wind veered in William's favour. Greatest luck of all, Harald Hardrada of Norway started an invasion of his own in Yorkshire, landing early in September. It was too much for the North Country *fyrd* to deal with. King Harold had to choose between the invasion which had started and the one which was only threatened and now looked as though it might never come. He rode northwards with his regular army, and, on 25th September, smashed the Norwegians at the Battle of Stamford Bridge. That was the moment when the wind changed in the Channel, and on 28th September William launched his own attack.

If he had been able to do so a few weeks earlier he would have met a fleet to dispute his crossing. And on the beaches he would have met the mass array of the *fyrd* from all the southern counties, Harold himself, and all the regular troops, under the golden standard of the Fighting Man. Or, if the wind had stayed contrary, for just a few more days, Harold would have been back from Yorkshire with his regulars at least, and time to call out the rest of his men. But it was not so. William sailed at dusk on Michaelmas Eve, not knowing until some time later the full total of his luck.

William led the fleet out from St. Valéry in his flagship, the *Mora*. Her name was appropriate, being the Latin for "delay". Her mast-head lantern guided the ships behind. Her figurehead was a golden boy, whose carved eyes gazed serenely across the darkling waters towards the invisible island.

How many ships spread their wings in the wake of the *Mora*? Some say there were three thousand—that William's half-brother, Odo, himself contributed a hundred—but this total sounds too large, even making full allowance for all the horses and equipment. The Norman army which fought at Hastings, two weeks later, numbered about nine thousand men. At all events, it was a great host, for those days—yet to William's dismay, when dawn came, he saw not another craft in view.

It was a hazy autumn morning. The shingly beach of Pevensey was near. William gave orders to anchor, and sent a ship's boy scrambling to the mast-head. At first the boy could see nothing, then he called down to say that the mist was lifting, and that a whole forest of masts could be seen. The *Mora* weighed anchor and ran forward into the land-locked harbour which now is the dry land of Pevensey Levels. Exultantly, William leapt ashore—only to stumble forward on hands and knees. Quick-witted, so that superstitious men should not be dismayed, he righted himself and held up his hands, clutching sand and shingle, turning the accident into a symbolic gesture of possession.

"By the Splendour of God," he roared, "I have taken *seizin* of England!"

By late afternoon the ships were beached, the army ashore, and the horses at grass. It would have been very different if Harold had been there. . . .

But Harold was two hundred miles away in Yorkshire. When the news reached him, he started south. Those men who could keep up with him did so. It was a business for mounted men, and well-mounted men at that. Possibly some foot-soldiers managed that prodigious march by hanging on to the stirrup-leathers of the horsemen. At any rate, Harold reached London within a week, gathered what fresh forces he could there, and hurtled on to meet the invaders. The last seventy miles was covered in three days. He reached Hastings with about the same number of men as William's, and further reinforcements trickled in, hour by hour. But whereas the Normans were fresh and all fighting men of good quality, the English ranged from the pick of the royal guard to the poorly-armed local levies. The better part of Harold's forces were tired by their almost-incredible march down the length of England, and before that they had been cruelly mauled by the Norwegians. Stamford Bridge, though a victory, had not been an easy one.

The Battle of Hastings raged throughout a whole October day. It was touch and go all the time. William knew he could lose. That was why he had never moved more than a mile or two from the escape-route offered by his ships.

There is no need to re-tell the familiar tale of that day, but two common statements need correcting. It is probably *not* true that the Normans led the English to break ranks by pretending to run away: most likely the Norman flight was genuine for the time being, but they recovered themselves and took advantage of the English mistake in following them. No one was trained for so difficult and well-disciplined a manœuvre as a pretended retreat plus recovery. Nor is it likely that William had a cunning idea and ordered his archers to shoot in the air with any special intention: the feeble little bows of the eleventh century (so very different from the six-foot weapon of Robin Hood) had to be pointed in the air anyhow, if their arrows were to fly any distance. In this case the English held the crest of a steep ridge, so William may have told his men to shoot even more steeply skywards. Certainly he could not have foreseen that one of the arrows— trivial, dart-like missiles compared with the clothyard shafts of Robin—would strike Harold full in the eye, and rob the English of their leader.

William's luck had stayed with him to the end.

His flagship had been named "Delay". And "Delay" was still his watchword.

Though the flower of the English army had died round their fallen king there were thousands of fighting men who had never reached Hastings. An Alfred could have rallied them and still thrown the Normans back into the sea. And if Harold had been a member of the ancient royal family, with a son or a brother to succeed him, England could have united and beaten William. But, as things were, could the English find any new leader and agree upon him?

William could not be sure. He dared not march straight on London and risk defeat. London was already so large a town that no army could surround it. That was to be true throughout English history: armies might grow, as the supply-problem became easier, but London always grew faster.

He took his time that autumn. He marched westwards in a wide, curving sweep, like a wolf prowling round the fold. He reached the Thames at Wallingford, far upstream. He devastated the countryside as he went, striking fear into the people. Given time to work on the fainter hearts, that fear would weaken his enemies' resistance. He crossed the Thames and swung round towards London again, cutting the roads to the north. The northern earls brought no help to the Londoners; they were playing for their own interests. So, at last, a delegation of bishops and nobles came out to William and offered him the crown. On Christmas Day, he was solemnly crowned King of England in Westminster Abbey.

There was hard fighting yet to be done. It took three or four years to master the country. There was a campaign in the West Country, where Harold's mother, Gytha, roused Devon and Dorset to resist him. There was revolt in the north, and a landing of Danes to aid the rebels. There was a killing winter march through the Pennines to smash the resistance of Chester. There was a last famous flickering of independence by Hereward in the Fens. William beat all his enemies, because they never joined together.

He was clever in keeping them disunited. True, he had to keep his promises to his followers and give them English lands. True, he was privately determined to put Normans into as many key-positions as he could. But he was careful never to behave like a foreign conqueror, with an open policy of favouring the outsider against the native.

He always insisted that he was King of England not by
conquest but by law. He had a sincere passion for law—
though often he paid more attention to the letter of it than
the spirit. No Englishman was to be put out of his lands
simply because he was English. If he lost his estates, it was
because he had rebelled against his lawful king. French or
English were to be treated exactly alike in the eyes of the
law, and it was English law. It just happened that most rebels
tended to be Englishmen. . . .

In the same way, though William was anxious to reform
the easy-going English Church, he did not turn out the
English bishops and put foreigners in their places. It just
happened that, as the English bishops died, the right men to
replace them proved to be foreigners. By the end of his
reign, there was not a single English bishop.

All this was a gradual process. There was no sudden edict,
hurting everyone at once and driving people to unite and
resist him. Each individual hoped that he might, personally,
be lucky. It was encouraging that William paid such close
heed to English law and custom, that he tried to learn English
himself (he was too busy to get far with it), and that he saw
to it that his youngest son Henry was taught the language.

Henry (afterwards Henry the First) was English born.
Matilda had followed William as soon as it was safe enough.
She had been made queen and was the first English king's
wife to add *Regina* to her signature. Saxon consorts had not
used the title. Henry was born at Selby in Yorkshire, two
years after Hastings. By then, Robert the eldest boy was
fourteen and William Rufus, the red-haired, was twelve.
Altogether they had three sisters, named Constance, Adela,
and Agatha. A big family, but not, as it turned out, a happy
one. William's sons grew up to plague him and almost break
his heart.

He was better at taming England. Year by year the loose,
free-and-easy kingdom became more firmly organised. He

was having no great barons defying him from petty kingdoms of their own: except on the Welsh and Scottish borders, where big forces were needed to keep out raiders, he arranged that his lords should hold estates scattered in different regions. All landowners, too, had to swear allegiance to him personally, as the king. They could not excuse disloyalty to him by saying that they had been obeying some intermediate overlord.

Twenty years after his accession, William carried his work of organisation a stage further. He had the idea of a systematic survey of the whole country's wealth and resources, village by village, down to the last acre. He announced this plan when he was spending Christmas at Gloucester Abbey—he followed the old tradition of the English kings and "wore his crown", in state, three times every year for the main Christian festivals. It was always Christmas at Gloucester, Easter at Winchester, and Whitsuntide at Westminster. His plan for the survey was put into effect and became the Domesday Book, the most complete record of its kind in medieval Europe and, for that reason, the envy of all foreign historians.

William changed the face of England in several ways.

When he came, there were only three castles in the whole country. He and his barons dotted the land with castles in the continental style. In every shire the peasants toiled to dig out moats and heap up huge mounds, which were topped at first with wooden towers and later with the stone keeps we associate with a Norman castle. William himself was responsible for the White Tower, in London, and the first castles at Windsor, Rochester, Nottingham, and a host of other key-points. Countless others were built by his barons.

New churches too began to rise, replacing older and smaller ones. Lanfranc was made Archbishop of Canterbury at the first opportunity. Within four years of Hastings, he had begun the rebuilding of the cathedral. Gundulf, a monk,

WILLIAM THE CONQUEROR

was brought over from Bec in Normandy and made Bishop of Rochester. He not only rebuilt his cathedral but also planned the keep of Dover Castle near-by. All the best architects were monks: William brought them over from France and even Italy. The distinctive features of Norman architecture began to spread everywhere—the round arch supported by short, massive columns, plain at base and capital, and the simple plastered walls. No stained glass relieved the severity of these churches; it did not reach England for another century.

In another, grimmer fashion William left his mark on the scene. He enlarged the hunting-grounds in Hampshire, turning out the peasants where necessary. He created the New Forest, little guessing that in years to come his son Rufus was to die there, victim of a mysterious arrow. Far worse in its consequences was his deliberate action in laying waste a vast tract of northern England, the "harrying of the north", as it was called. Its object was to weaken Northumberland so that it should not rebel against him a second time: its result was to leave that district so weak and poor that it scarcely recovered itself until the modern age of coal and iron.

William was a strange blend of mercy and cruelty. It is not fair to judge him by twentieth-century standards.

He sentenced many men to be maimed—blinded or deprived of a limb—but it was a common punishment in those days and it was considered more merciful than the death-penalty. It was William's pride that, apart from those killed in battle, he was responsible for hardly any man's death. He made great efforts, too, to stop the slave-trade between Ireland and the ports of western England.

He was certainly a much milder ruler than his half-brother Odo. Unfortunately for the English, Odo was far too often left in charge as regent. For William divided his time fairly equally between England and Normandy. Matilda, after that first year or two, lived almost entirely in Normandy. It was in these later years that she and her ladies are said to have embroidered the Bayeux tapestry, telling the story of the Conquest in what we should now call "strip" form. The tapestry is of linen, 220 feet long by 20 inches wide, the figures being worked in woollen threads in eight different colours. As the work was done with needles, it is not strictly a tapestry at all.

William's last years were dark. The splendid adventure of the Conquest had been successful, he had won over the majority of his new subjects, he had found an outlet for his tremendous energies and organising powers—but there was a strange emptiness in victory.

His sons were a disappointment. Robert especially, whom he planned to make Duke of Normandy but not King of England. They quarrelled and fought, Matilda showed too much sympathy for her son, and husband and wife had their first serious difference since the far-off day of their tempestuous courtship. Then Matilda died and was buried, magnificently, in the abbey at Caen. William was alone.

He was an elderly man now, by the standards of that century, though still on the right side of sixty. The dark hair had thinned to baldness, the once athletic figure had thickened and coarsened into fat. But he rode on, wearily and without zest, and fought more battles against his unruly subjects in Maine or border raiders from the French king's territory.

It was these raiders that took him to Mantes, a town near the edge of Normandy. It was August, 1087. He had taken a harsh revenge upon the raiders. The town was a smouldering ruin. He had always believed in firm measures . . . just punishments. . . .

Suddenly his tired charger stumbled. He was thrown sharply against the pommel of his saddle and suffered an internal injury. He could not remount, so they carried him out of the town to the abbey of St. Gervais. There he lingered for several weeks, and died on the 9th September. The doctors who had failed to save him fled in panic, the nobles (fearing rebellions and civil war) rode off to prepare themselves for any emergency, and the servants took their chance to loot the building. Even the dead man's robes and bed-linen were taken. William lay deserted and almost naked on the floor.

Of the Conqueror, as of all men, the words of the burial service rang true: "*We brought nothing into this world, and it is certain we can carry nothing out.*"

THE YEARS BETWEEN 1087–1157

ONLY a man's lifetime, the Bible's threescore years and ten, lies between the death of the Conqueror and the birth of his great-great-grandson, Richard I. But in that short space there had been many changes. The strong fingers of the Normans had moulded England to a new shape. Able and energetic kings (none more so than Richard's own father, Henry II) had brought more efficient government. Gone was the old, easy-going Saxon spirit, in Church as well as in State. Bishops and abbots of the stern Norman pattern vied with the King's officers and the barons to ensure that the rank-and-file did their duty as they should. Both the medieval church and the feudal system had reached the fullest pitch of their organisation.

There were other changes to the outward eye. True, the pattern of the fields, the peasants' hovels, the spreading miles of forest, were unaltered. But the age of castle-building started by the Conqueror had continued, and now every shire had a newish-looking stone fortress or two, crowning the more conspicuous hillocks. Most of the little Saxon churches and cathedrals had been scornfully demolished and rebuilt more magnificently, often in part with stone shipped from Normandy. Monasteries had expanded and multiplied; no friars had yet reached England, but monks and nuns were active as farmers, teachers, nurses, and in many other ways. The towns were beginning to grow as crafts and trades developed. The square yellow cap of the Jew was seen more often bobbing among the round caps and pointed hoods of the Christian crowd.

3

Richard: The Crusader

RICHARD—destined to be known to later ages as *Coeur-de-Lion* or "Lion-heart"—was born at Oxford on 8th September, 1157.

Oxford was then a small town. It had never fully recovered from a disastrous fire about a century before—Domesday Book registers half the houses as in ruins—and although scholars had begun to gather there it was to be another hundred years before the first college was founded. There was a traditional curse on any King of England entering the city, and that is no doubt why Richard's parents had their palace at Beaumont.

No trace of that palace remains, except the name, Beaumont Street, now a busy thoroughfare with theatre and museum, close to the heart of the city. But when Richard saw the light of day Beaumont Palace was well outside the Oxford boundary, perhaps a bow-shot from where, very soon, the northern wall of the town was to be built.

Richard was the remarkable son of equally remarkable parents.

His father, Henry the Second, was one of the strongest of the medieval English kings, as he needed to be to restore order after the long civil war between his mother Queen Maud and his uncle King Stephen.

He was a powerfully-built man, with a big freckled face and short reddish hair. His energy was as terrifying as his hot temper. He could out-walk and out-ride his courtiers, and frequently exhausted them. "He never sits down," lamented one of them, "he is always on his feet from morning till night." Even his meals were often taken standing, and court etiquette therefore prevented everyone else from sitting. Even in church he was so restless that he whispered frequently to his neighbours, or doodled. His voice, always harsh and cracked, became almost hysterical when passion seized him. The most momentous of these outbursts was the one which caused four of his knights to rush off and murder Thomas-à-Becket at Canterbury. Altogether, an alarming parent even for a Lion-heart to possess.

Richard's mother, Queen Eleanor, was herself formidable. Long years later, at the age of eighty-four, she stood a siege on behalf of her youngest son, King John. One cannot help wondering how she got on with her mother-in-law, the even more formidable Queen-Empress Maud.*

Eleanor had been Queen of France before, and, if she told Richard only a tenth of her experiences (she certainly could not have told him all), he must have had an entertaining childhood. She was a gay, frivolous society woman, as fantastic in her dress as King Henry was simple in his. But, she must have assured Richard, she was not empty-headed, she cared deeply for the things of the spirit. Why, in her younger days at the French Court, she had not only heard the renowned Bernard preach the second Crusade but she had been so moved by his eloquence that she had taken the Cross herself!

Sitting at her feet, the future adversary of Saladin listened (we can only guess with what private thoughts) to his mother's carefully edited account of her own adventures in the Holy Land. How she and her ladies had put on armour and drilled in public. How they had scornfully sent their distaffs to those knights of their acquaintance who had not yet volunteered to fight the Saracens. How they had set off

* For her story, see *The Seven Queens of England*.

for Palestine with an immense armament, not forgetting tents of gold-embroidered silk, cushions, and a fashionable wardrobe for off-duty moments. What interesting places they had seen, and what delightful (or impossible) people they had met during the long journey across Europe.

And what about the fighting, any boy must have asked with some impatience, and certainly a boy of Richard's type. Well . . . At this point we may imagine that his mother became a trifle evasive. The Crusaders had, in fact, been soundly beaten by the Saracens. Eleanor and her ladies had made a dramatic escape, her then husband, King Louis, had saved himself by climbing a tree, but the silken tents and cushions had been abandoned, along with most of their clothes and all hope of delivering Jerusalem from the infidel.

And what happened then? Eleanor may well have smiled at her memories. She had gone to Antioch, where the handsome young Raymond of Poitou was king. He was, actually, her uncle, but that had not prevented her flirting with him. There had been other admirers too. Eleanor, with her hot southern blood, could never resist the temptations of a love-affair. There had even been a forward young emir of thirteen, a wicked Saracen, of course, but strangely attractive. . . .

She was a married woman, of course. But—was she? She had begun to wonder. If you pored long enough over the family-trees of European royalties, you found that she and King Louis were fourth cousins. Strictly speaking they should never have married. Strictly speaking they were *not* married. Modern divorce was unknown in the Middle Ages, but the rich and powerful had nearly always another device in reserve, the excuse of a forgotten family-relationship.

Back in Paris, Eleanor's doubts had grown stronger, from the moment when she met Geoffrey the Handsome, the young husband of the Empress Maud. She had fallen madly in love with him, but he had died. When his son, Henry, came to Paris, she fell in love with him instead. Her marriage with

King Louis was dissolved, and that, Eleanor may have concluded, "was how I married your dear father".

They had certainly not lived happily ever after. It would have been strange if they had, two such difficult and different characters. King Henry was fifteen years younger than his queen, and later he was to have his own unlawful connection with the Fair Rosamund de Clifford, at Woodstock not far from Oxford. A legend was to grow up that he had kept Rosamund hidden in a maze, and that Eleanor found her way in by using a thread, as in the Greek legend, and poisoned her rival. The fact is that Eleanor, by then, had so fallen out with Henry that she was kept under arrest and let out only when it was absolutely essential that she should appear in public as Queen beside her husband.

These events were still in the future when Richard was small. He had a brother, Henry, two years older, and another, Geoffrey, a year younger than himself. When he was ten another boy was born, also at Beaumont Palace, that John who was one day to grant the Magna Carta. And there were three sisters in all, Maud, Eleanor, and Joan.

Richard was his mother's favourite. None of the boys liked their father, though John, being much the youngest, did not come out in open rebellion. Richard had a special link with his mother, for it was planned that he should eventually inherit the rich French duchy of Aquitaine, which was her own family possession. Aquitaine comprised the southern third of France, including the romantic region of the troubadours.

Perhaps it was from his mother that Richard first learnt to love music and poetry. We know that later his friends included such famous minstrels as Blondel de Nesle and Bertrand de Born, and that he composed songs both in French and in Provençal. In his private chapel, far from whispering or doodling as his father had done, he used to walk up and down conducting the choir.

·   ·   ·   ·   ·

Richard's childhood was full of colour and movement. His mother brought the brilliance of Southern France to the English court, and that court was itself continually travelling from castle to castle, or crossing the narrow seas to the Continent, for, what with her own vast Duchy of Aquitaine and King Henry's territories in Normandy, Maine, and Anjou, the English royal family controlled the greater part of what is France today.

Richard's early memories were therefore divided between the two countries. There was a gay Christmas at Marlborough Castle when he was seven: the last time he saw his mother rule the revels of a really happy English family Christmas. After that, the clouds began to gather round his parents' marriage. The next May, his mother took him to Normandy, with his elder sister, to join his father who had gone before them. The King was by then in the midst of his fateful quarrel with Becket, and even a seven year old boy could feel that the atmosphere was heavier than usual.

There were, of course, returns to England—returns to the very palace where he was born, and where, ten years later, a brother was born, to be christened John. Richard had always a strong affection for this younger brother: even when John was treacherous to him, Richard would always forgive. It was natural to feel protective towards him as the baby of the family, the late, last son whom his father somewhat cruelly nicknamed "Lackland" because there was no inheritance left to promise him. John's reddish, curly head never came much above Richard's shoulder—as men they were five foot six and six foot two respectively—but what John lacked in height he made up for in sly humour and charm. Richard was amused by John and sorry for him, especially when his name was put down for admission as a monk at Fontevrault Abbey. John made it clear, as he grew older, that he was not suited to the monkish life, and no further attempt was made to force him into it.

Richard's thoughts were now less on Oxford and England than on the sunny realm of Aquitaine. That was where his future was planned to lie. When he was eleven, he went with his father and elder brother to meet the King of France at Montmirail. There was an impressive ceremonial of "doing homage", for in theory even King Henry acknowledged a kind of French overlordship so far as his continental lands were concerned. When he had thus paid homage, Richard's elder brother Henry knelt and paid homage for Britanny, Anjou and Maine. Finally it was Richard's turn, for the Duchy of Aquitaine.

When this was completed, Richard was solemnly betrothed to the French princess, Aloysia, King Louis' daughter by a second marriage. As the young couple were still only children, there was no question of a wedding for some years.

More to Richard's taste was the ceremony, just before his fifteenth birthday, when he was installed as Duke in the abbey church of St. Hilary at Poitiers. He was enthroned in the abbot's chair. The sacred lance and banner of the dukedom were placed in his hands by the Archbishop of Bordeaux and the Bishop of Poitiers. Later he went on to Limoges, where a great procession came to meet him. The holy ring of St. Valeria the martyr was put upon his finger, and all the people shouted, acclaiming him as their new duke.

Richard had come into his heritage, it seemed. But it was an uneasy one. Duke he might be, but he was still under the guardianship of his mother—and by now the split between his parents was open. Eleanor was plotting against King Henry, and she persuaded her three elder sons to side with her. First young Henry fled from his father's side in Normandy and went to King Louis. Then Richard and his younger brother Geoffrey went from Aquitaine to join him. John was still too much of a child to be involved.

In Paris they swore a solemn oath. They would not desert the French king or make any separate peace with their father.

Louis, in turn, would help the young Henry to the throne of England.

It is very hard for the modern mind to understand these medieval family-feuds. The first thing to realise is that the fathers and sons in conflict were not trying to kill one another. Thus, on a later occasion when Richard's forces were chasing his father's out of a blazing town, Richard galloped forward without any arms and at great risk to his life, simply to make sure that no personal hurt was done to his father.

The mentality of the people quarrelling can be imagined best in terms of a gigantic family row, magnified by the size of the inheritances involved, by the strong passions of the various individuals, which they were not accustomed to control, and by the fact that each was backed by a band of supporters and sympathisers. To these men war was a sport. A campaign, with a few skirmishes, was scarcely more dangerous than a hard season of modern foxhunting, with its several days a week throughout the winter. If taken prisoner, you were politely treated and then ransomed: so, even to the enemy, you were more useful alive than dead. War was hardest on the lower classes: their houses and fields suffered, and, if they were among the fighting-men, they were more likely to be killed since they were not worth ransoming. Their point of view was not always forgotten, but it was seldom allowed to spoil the game for their rulers.

At sixteen Richard was knighted by King Louis and was henceforth fully qualified to share in the sport of chivalry. He still did not marry Aloysia. Indeed, the engagement dragged on for years, but it was a political one and in the end, for political reasons, never came to anything.

The details of the civil wars and rebellions, sometimes between Henry the Second and his sons, sometimes between Richard and his brothers, sometimes between Richard and his various French opponents, matter no more than the scores of last year's football matches. But Richard could claim, as a man, that he had learnt his soldiering in the field, and that his skill in arms was acquired in battle, not in mock-fights and tournaments. He was only twenty-one when he established himself as a general of the first rank, by capturing the fortress of Taillebourg, which had never been taken before and was considered impregnable. Richard took it after a ten-day siege, and razed it to the ground.

His mother had by then lost her leading position in the family-feud. In the first year of the revolt against King Henry she had been captured while trying to reach the French King's territory in disguise—some said, wrapped in a nun's habit, others that she was dressed as a man and riding astride. At any rate, from that time onwards, the King kept her under control.

When Richard was twenty-five, his elder brother died. This made him heir to the English crown. His father suggested that he should hand over some of his Aquitaine inheritance to John, and, when he refused, encouraged John to make war against his brother. But Richard was always able to deal with John, and ready to forgive him afterwards.

Just at this time Richard met Berengaria, daughter of King Sancho of Navarre, the little Spanish kingdom at the western end of the Pyrenees. He was attracted to her, but he was still supposed to be engaged to the French princess.

Two years later his younger brother, Geoffrey, died. King Henry's unmanageable sons were now reduced to two—and of these John kept up a show of obedience to his father almost until the end.

Late the next year tremendous news burst over Christendom, which altered the whole of Richard's life.

Since the First Crusade, Jerusalem had been the capital of a Christian kingdom, and the holy places and relics had been safe for pilgrims to visit. Now a new Saracen leader had arisen in Saladin. He had defeated the Christians, captured their king, Guy of Lusignan, and seized the Cross itself, the most sacred relic of all. It had been sent to Baghdad and buried under the threshold of the city gate, so that every passer-by should tread it underfoot.

The news reached Richard one November evening at Tours. He was a religious man and a fighter. He needed no emotional sermon to stir his blood. First thing the next morning he went to an archbishop and vowed to go on another Crusade, to rescue the holy city and, God willing, the Cross as well.

Such ventures could not be planned in a moment. The very news, sensational though it was, had taken several months to reach France. Now it was necessary to collect money, men and ships. The scheme was nothing less than a sea-borne invasion on a grand scale at the far side of the then-known world. Richard was still preparing for it, more than eighteen months later, when another piece of important news reached him; this also, by a coincidence, at Tours.

His father was dead. He was now King Richard the First of England.

His first act was to hurry to the funeral at Fontevraud. His next, to send word to England, ordering the release of his mother, and appointing her to govern until he could arrive. Only after three weeks did he cross the Channel. His mother met him at Winchester, with all the chief bishops and barons. He was given a warm welcome, not least from the common people.

All people under arrest for offences against the Forest Law were released. All men outlawed for the same reason could return to their homes without fear. Many other offenders were set free and pardoned. After the efficient but harsh justice of Henry II a milder breeze of forgiveness was blowing across the land. John shared in it. Richard was ready to let bygones be bygones.

He was not forgetting his Crusader's vow. If he devoted

himself for the moment to his new kingdom it was because he knew that, as king, he would be better able to fit out an expedition.

On the other hand, in pushing forward with his plan, he did not feel that he was neglecting England. His father had organised the government so well that, for the first time in history, it could be trusted to run smoothly when the king's back was turned. Richard personally knew little of this country which he had never until recently expected to rule.

Above all, Richard was vowed to the Crusade, and he was a man of his word. Not for nothing had his troubadour friend, Bertrand de Born, nicknamed him *Richard Oc-e-No*, "Richard Yea-and-Nay", meaning that his yes was yes, and his no was no. Richard seldom swore oaths in daily matters, as other men did. A simple statement or promise was enough.

The Crusades meant very different things to different people. They had meant fashionable excitement to his mother. To many—landless knights and cut-throat adventurers— they meant the chance of loot, perhaps even the carving out of new estates and kingdoms in captured territory. Such men cared little whether they robbed the Saracens or their fellow-Christians in Eastern Europe. To ship-owners, again, to contractors and business men of all kinds, a Crusade was a golden opportunity to make quick profits.

Richard was perhaps one of the few who undertook the venture without selfish motives.

But first, on 3rd September, 1189, just before his thirty-second birthday, there was another solemn oath which even Richard Yea-and-Nay took willingly: the threefold Coronation oath, to maintain the peace of the Church, to suppress injustice, and to promote equity and mercy.

This coronation, in Westminster Abbey, is a landmark in the history of the ceremony, for it was used as a model at all coronations afterwards.

Richard made a knightly figure as he stood before the altar

and was solemnly arrayed in the robes of his great office. Few men present could remember any English king but Henry—and Henry, though powerful and athletic, had been anything but romantic with his bow legs, his cropped, thinning hair, and his florid complexion.

The new king was tall and carried his chin high. He had the long straight legs which, when repeated in a later ruler, Edward I, gave that king the nickname, "Longshanks". His features were fine and regular: not for nothing was he the son of the lovely Eleanor of Aquitaine and the grandson, on the other side, of Geoffrey the Handsome, of Anjou. His hair was of the reddish-gold that was common in the Plantagenet family, and he wore a close-trimmed beard. His complexion was fair, his eyes blue, with a sparkle that could blaze into anger when his pride or his beliefs were touched.

The coronation service was followed by three days of solemn festivities, carried out with more decorum than usual. No ladies were allowed at the banquets and the clergy were given the seats of honour. Jews also were barred from the proceedings. There were, of course, no Jews among the nobility. Being unable to take a Christian oath, they were unable to hold land: and as Christians were not supposed to lend money at interest (and were naturally unwilling to lend it for nothing), the Jews had been more or less driven to banking as an occupation. Richard was not himself anti-Jewish, but he felt that his coronation was, first and foremost, a Christian rite.

Unfortunately, some Jews went to the palace doors on the first evening, bearing gifts for him. They were set upon by the ignorant mob and driven away. Richard, hearing the noise outside, sent some of his officers to see what was the matter, but they were too late to do anything. A savage anti-Jewish riot had begun and swept through London. Jews were murdered and their houses looted. As in Eastern cities in our own century, there were always plenty of people ready to turn a political or a religious riot into an opening for theft or personal revenge.

Richard was grieved that his coronation should have been marred in this way. It was impossible to find and punish the guilty, but he at once sent orders to every part of England that the Jews should be left in peace. So long as he remained in the country there was no more persecution.

As a king of England Richard has almost no historical importance: of his ten years' reign he spent less than ten months in his kingdom. In one thing only he affected its future, and that was by accident.

As the medieval towns grew in size they all had one ambition—to win their freedom from the local landowner (it might be a baron or a monastery) who had ruled local affairs when they were mere villages. Such a landowner could levy tolls on their markets, and, in one way or another, skim the cream off their increasing prosperity. So what every town wanted was a charter from the King, giving it the right to control its own affairs. All through the Middle Ages we see this struggle between the middle-class townsmen and the landed nobility or the Church authorities.

Richard was not interested in the development of local government, but he was interested in money for the Crusade. He was prepared to seal any number of charters if the towns would buy them from him. "I would sell London," he cried, "if I could find a buyer." It was just because he was more interested in the Crusade than in his kingdom that, without realising it, he cleared the road for the English towns to move forward.

Some say that Richard was equally ready to sell public offices, and even bishoprics, to the highest bidder, but this is not entirely true. He did gather donations from men he appointed, but he did not always choose the man who offered most, if he was not also the most suitable.

Just before Christmas he left for Normandy. The Crusade was to start in the spring. He was to be joined in it by the King of France, now Philip Augustus. Bishop William of Ely was to govern England in his absence, with the rank of Chief Justiciar. Brother John, though provided for with ample lands and income, was not to interfere.

For months Richard had been busy enrolling men and commandeering ships and horses. The English vessels were to make the long voyage from their home ports, via Gibraltar, to Marseilles. Here Richard would embark with the army he had brought overland through France, from his assembly-point at Tours. The crossing of the Mediterranean to the port of Acre, in Syria, could be made in fifteen days.

Tours, the old town by the Loire, was humming with activity. Knights and men-at-arms, crossbow-men and siege-engineers, armourers and farriers, grooms and camp-followers of every kind, poured in to enrol under the banner of the Lion-heart. Here, in the same town where he had taken the Cross, and from the same archbishop's hands, Richard received the symbolic staff of a pilgrim. He leant on it, testing it, and it broke under his weight. Those who believed in omens wondered if that boded ill-luck for the whole venture.

Philip Augustus and his army joined Richard for the march down the Rhone valley. Then, to ease the problems of food and transport and billets, they divided again. Philip preferred a shorter sea-trip within safe reach of the Italian coast, so he made for Genoa. His main body, lacking ships, went by land down the length of Italy. The two kings were to meet again and concentrate their forces at Messina in Sicily.

Richard's ships were late. After a week he refused to stay at Marseilles any longer. So, as the old record says (quaintly sounding, to modern ears), he "hired two large busses and twenty well-armed galleys" and set off. In the twelfth century a "buss" was a transport-ship, with one large square sail.

Any idea of a fifteen-day passage to Syria had by now been abandoned. Exact time-schedules were impossible. There were a hundred and one factors to cause delay. Sincere though Richard was in his desire to reach the Holy Land it was, in fact, not fifteen days but ten months that passed, from the day he set out from Marseilles until the day he landed in Syria.

He took his time, coasting down the west of Italy, knowing that his fleet had still to overtake him at Messina. Growing tired of the slow-moving, uncomfortable ships, he went ashore and did a good deal of sightseeing round Naples, though he refused the Pope's invitation to visit Rome. Riding down through Calabria he got himself into a village brawl, through trying to seize a falcon which had taken his fancy. The peasants went for him with sticks and stones, and Richard threw stones back at them. The trouble was probably due to language-difficulty, for Richard was open-handed and probably meant to offer a generous price for the bird. He deliberately refrained from using more than the flat of his sword, and, finding that he could not beat off his attackers, without badly hurting them, he was not too proud to run away.

He spent more than six months in Sicily. There were all kinds of matters to be settled. His sister Joan was there: she had been married to the King of Sicily, who had recently died, and there was her future to be arranged. There were questions to be discussed with the French king: was Richard, or was he not, going to marry Princess Aloysia? The answer to this question was brought by Queen Eleanor who, despite her great age, arrived in Italy with Princess Berengaria. Richard announced that he would marry Berengaria, and the engagement to Aloysia was finally broken. Queen Eleanor started briskly back, after staying a mere four days, and the Spanish princess remained behind with Richard's sister as chaperone.

These and other matters occupied the winter. The delay was unavoidable anyhow. Sea-captains did not sail during the winter if they could help it: neither the ships nor the seamanship of those days were good enough. With great fleets and convoys it would have been suicide to face the open sea in the bad season; and when Richard did at last put forth from the harbour of Messina, on 10th April, it was with a positive armada.

First went three great busses, or dromonds as they were called in the Mediterranean. In one of these sailed Queen Joan, leaving her late husband's kingdom, and with her went Berengaria, sometimes known as "the Damsel of Navarre".

Behind them, line after line, and each line longer than the one in front, glided the rest of the fleet—first thirteen ships, then fourteen, twenty, thirty, forty, seventy—a mighty arrowhead, aimed at the coast of Syria. The last line consisted of war-galleys, the rest were dromonds or smaller transportvessels called ushers, tub-like craft without oars. A dromond carried forty knights and their warhorses, forty foot-soldiers and a crew of fifteen sailors, together with arms and armour, a whole year's food and forage, and a portion of Richard's treasure. For fear of shipwreck, he had divided it among the fleet. An usher held about half as much as a dromond. One of the biggest items in the loading plan was the spare horse taken for every knight in the army. Richard knew that spare horses were essential in such a hot climate, when riders were so heavily armoured. All these horses, and their fodder, had to be fitted in somewhere.

As soon as the armada had cleared the Straits of Messina, Richard and his war-galleys put on speed and moved up to the head of the convoy. Richard was at home aboard ship. Though his experience of the sea had gone little further than the occasional Channel crossing, he showed himself an

D

efficient commodore. "As a hen leads her chickens out to feed," wrote one chronicler, "he led his mighty fleet." Each vessel kept within hailing distance of its neighbours, each line was within trumpet-signal of those in front and behind it. The escort galleys adjusted their speed to that of the slower craft and the flagship, with a bright lantern shining after dark, set the course for all. Richard was not seasick like many of his followers, and the dirtiest weather did not affect his high spirits.

And certainly there was dirty weather enough. A tiresome calm gave place to contrary winds and then to a storm. The ships tossed and rolled, the oarsmen fighting to control their long oars, the horses stamping and whinnying in terror. The neat lines of vessels sagged and buckled. When daylight returned, Richard found he had lost touch with twenty-five of them, including the dromond which held Berengaria and his sister. He steered for the island of Rhodes, just off the mainland of Asia, but, though he waited hopefully there for three days, the missing ships did not arrive.

Some of them were in fact, at that moment, meeting fresh dangers off the south coast of another island, Cyprus. This large island was much further east. It was the last stepping-stone on the long journey to the Holy Land. It was supposed to be part of the Eastern Empire, and so Christian, but actually its governor, Isaac Comnenus, had set himself up as an independent "emperor". He paid no heed to his distant master in Byzantium, and was more inclined to help the Saracens than the Crusaders.

Two ships were wrecked on the rocks as they tried to enter the harbour of Limasol. The ship containing Queen Joan and Berengaria swung about, just in time, and rode out the bad weather in the open sea. When at last they were able to make port, they dared not land. Isaac had seized those Crusaders who had scrambled ashore from the wreck and only by great courage had they fought their way to freedom.

Now, with soft words and handsome presents, he tried to lure the ladies ashore. At last, with many misgivings, they told him they would land the next day.

Luckily, Richard's galley appeared before they could do so, with the rest of the fleet dotting the sea in his wake. His polite inquiry brought an insulting answer from the self-appointed emperor. Isaac mustered all his forces and drew them up behind a barricade at the water's edge. Richard ordered his knights and crossbowmen into the boats and led the landing-party himself. The air hissed and sang with arrows and bolts. The Crusaders were at a disadvantage, packed tight in the little boats and unprotected against their hidden enemies. Man after man slumped wounded over the gunwale. The knights were helpless, the archers had scarcely elbow-room to level their crossbows and no clear target to aim at. But, as the water grew shallower, Richard leapt out and waded ashore, brandishing his sword. His men followed. The Cypriots deserted their barricade. Isaac galloped off on his famous bay Arab, Fauvel. Richard seized a baggage-horse, with a sackcloth saddle and rope stirrups, and on this make-shift charger he thundered after his enemy, challenging him to "come and joust". Isaac did not even pause to acknowledge the invitation.

Richard made sure of the town and then got his horses ashore. First thing the next morning he pushed inland with a patrol of fifty horsemen, and found himself suddenly looking down upon Isaac's camp.

One of his companions turned to him—Hugh de la Mare, a secretary who had donned arms to join the patrol. "Come away, sire," he begged, "their numbers are too over-whelming."

"Get you to your own writing-business, sir clerk," the King answered. "Leave matters of chivalry to us!"

He was not going to lose the advantage of a surprise, and he knew that the main body of Crusaders was not far behind.

He ordered the charge, and the little band of knights swept down the hill. Richard himself made for Isaac's standard. The emperor escaped, but his standard-bearer went down, and Richard plucked the gold-embroidered flag from his hands. The rest of the Crusaders arrived before the Cypriots could rally, and there was a six-mile chase before the enemy found refuge in their native hills.

The ladies had by now landed in Limasol, and there, on 12th May, in a dim little chapel of the Norman fortress, Richard and Berengaria were married. They had intended to wait until they reached the Holy Land, but the journey was proving so much longer and so much more adventurous than they had expected that it seemed better to postpone their union no longer. After the wedding, the bride was immediately crowned Queen of England. Berengaria was not only remarkable in celebrating her coronation so far from Westminster, she was fated to be the only Queen of England who never set foot in the country.

While the festivities were still going on, Isaac asked for a peace-conference. Richard rode out and met him in an orchard of fig trees, close to the sea-shore. Richard was gloriously arrayed in a tunic of rose-coloured samite or silk. Over it was a great cloak of silver tissue, covered with half moons of solid silver and blazing suns. His cap was scarlet, his spurs and sword-hilt golden, his scabbard chased with silver. He rode a fine Spanish charger, to rival the emperor's Fauvel, and on his saddle were two rampant lion-cubs in gold, snarling at each other.

Once more, Richard was by no means wasting time by these dealings with Isaac. Cyprus was a convenient base— almost an essential base—for the food-supplies of any army invading the Holy Land. Cyprus must be made safe for the Crusade. Isaac's double dealings with the Saracens must be stopped.

The two kings duly met and Richard stated his demands.

RICHARD COEUR-DE-LION

Isaac pretended to agree, and promised to serve under Richard in the Crusade, with five hundred knights. But at the first opportunity, after they had exchanged the kiss of peace, he slipped out of the tent, mounted Fauvel, and fled once more. There was further fighting. A bout of fever hindered Richard, but, in spite of everything, it took him only fifteen days all told to complete the conquest of Cyprus.

The slippery Isaac grovelled before him, at the end, begging that at least he should not be put in irons. Richard agreed with a contemptuous curl of his lip—and then ordered that fetters of solid silver should be made for him. Isaac was handed over to the Knights Hospitallers, and died three years later in their fortress at Markab, near Mount Lebanon. Richard kept Fauvel for his own use. Then, with Berengaria, he embarked again. At last the way was clear to the Holy Land.

The French king had arrived six weeks before him and had taken charge of the siege of Acre, which had already been in progress for a long time. Saladin was not in the city. He lay in the hills outside, with his army of quick-moving, light-armed horsemen, harassing the Crusaders from the rear.

Richard brought new life to the siege. He was an expert both on fortification and on siege-methods. He had brought giant catapults with him—he had brought even the stones for them to hurl, special flinty stones from Sicily which burst into deadly fragments as they crashed over the enemy battlements. Even when he was struck down by malaria, he had himself carried round the trenches on a stretcher, loosing off an occasional bolt from his crossbow. He was a fine shot, and he never disdained any form of military service. When need arose, he would labour with his hands like the roughest pioneer.

Acre surrendered. The garrison marched out as prisoners. One of the conditions was that Saladin should hand over the Cross, which, contrary to the original report which had maddened Richard, had not been sent to Baghdad but was in safe, respectful keeping. Saladin allowed some of the Crusaders to inspect it, under flag of truce. But he did not give it up by the appointed date, nor did he confirm the rest of the agreement that his garrison had made. The Crusaders would not set free such a host of prisoners and they could not spare men to guard them. They therefore carried out a sickening cold-blooded massacre of the Saracens. Richard, as joint-leader of the Crusade, must bear a great share of the guilt. But the action did not shock the people of his own day. Not one of the chroniclers wrote a word of criticism, and even his enemy, Saladin, continued to admire him as the soul of chivalry. The twelfth-century eye saw the action as just.

Richard won more bitter hatred from his fellow-Crusader, the Duke of Austria, who had planted his banner on one of the towers in the sector allotted to the King. Richard had it pulled down and trampled on. The Duke never forgave him, and waited for his chance of revenge. Such was the mental outlook of chivalry.

The campaign-plan now fell into two parts. First, a southward march of seventy miles, down the narrow strip between the hills and the sea, to the port of Jaffa. Second, a right-angle turn and a thrust inland to Jerusalem.

The plan was doomed to failure. King Philip had already seen enough fighting. He was well satisfied with the capture of Acre. He sent messengers to beg Richard to release him from his vow: the Frenchmen delivered their message with tears of shame in their eyes. Richard could not keep such a reluctant ally. He rode on with his own forces alone.

After fierce fighting and terrible hardships he battled to within sight of the city he had come to deliver. But he refused to look, from that distant hill-top, upon a place which he now had to admit he could never capture, so long as Saladin was alive. A treaty of peace was made, and Richard, again racked with fever, was carried aboard his ship.

"Oh, Holy Land," he groaned as the coast grew dim in the

distance, "I commend thee to God. May He of His mercy grant me life to bring thee aid. For it is my hope and resolve, by His good will, to come back."

Like Odysseus of old, Richard found his return journey quite as adventurous as the outward voyage.

Berengaria and Joan had gone ahead by another route. Romantic in other ways, the Lion-heart was not an ardent lover. He had seen little of his wife during the campaign—that was understandable—and now he was content to travel separately and, as it turned out, they by no means hastened to each other's arms when at last it was possible to meet again.

Richard's choice of a route home has puzzled many. It is supposed that, when he recovered from his most recent bout of illness, he was bored and depressed by the failure of the Crusade. He went looking for trouble, and in that, at least, he was brilliantly successful.

When the facts are studied, Richard's route seems more sensible, though he was certainly foolhardy in some of the things he did.

He began by making for Marseilles. Then he got word that his enemies in France were plotting to seize him when he landed, and that King Philip himself favoured the scheme. Richard's great army was now disbanded, he was travelling with only a few personal companions, and he was not going to step into an obvious trap.

He could have turned towards Gibraltar and sailed straight to England. But it was now November, and a dangerous season for the Bay of Biscay. He therefore decided to travel by the easterly land route, through Austria and Germany. He overlooked the little matter of the trampled banner at Acre. He forgot that he had an Austrian enemy as bitter as any in France.

He changed course and sailed up the Adriatic to Corfu. Three galleys lay off the island. Richard put out in a small boat and hailed them. They were pirate-craft and answered him with a volley of arrows. The King then congratulated them on their fighting spirit, and suggested that they should carry him and his staff to the port of Ragusa, now Dubrovnik in Yugoslavia, for a payment of two hundred silver marks.

The bargain was not so crazy as it sounds. The Adriatic was a perilous sea and its rocky coasts offered few places of refuge. There could be no safer pilot than a local pirate. And, if there was any treachery, Richard and his knights would not have been easy passengers to overcome. Even the pirates could see that, for this one trip at least, honesty was the best policy.

Richard's common sense was shown when they ran into such a violent storm that, with all their seamanship and local knowledge, the pirates barely managed to avoid shipwreck. Richard vowed that, if only they came safe to land, he would spend a hundred thousand ducats on building a church at that spot. Finally he got ashore on a rocky island just outside the port of Ragusa. After some hesitation, and with the Pope's approval for the slight alteration in his vow, Richard spent most of the money on rebuilding the cathedral in Ragusa itself. But the Benedictine monks on the island were not forgotten, and their own little church was rebuilt as well.

Voyaging on, when he had seen the work started, Richard ran into another storm. This time his ship was actually wrecked, and he struggled ashore somewhere in the Gulf of Venice. At this point he wisely decided that he was not equipped to travel in state as the King of England. He would be too tempting a prey to possible enemies. "A king's ransom" was not an empty phrase in the twelfth century. It was a golden dream which, once in a while, a bold enough villain might turn into reality.

So Richard disguised himself as "Hugh the merchant", a pilgrim returning from the Holy Land, and sent word to the Count of Gorizia near-by, asking for safe-conduct. Wisely

he backed his request with a present: unwisely—forgetting
that merchants did not make presents quite on the royal scale
—he sent a ruby ring of considerable value.

"His name is not Hugh," said the Count as he studied the
gift. "It is Richard, the King."

He promised the safe-conduct but Richard, knowing that
his secret was out, took no further chances. Buying horses,
he and his friends started off in the middle of the night. The
Count chased after them and captured eight. Richard and
the rest slipped through the Alps into Carinthia, but there
was now a regular hue and cry after them.

At Freisach the local baron had a servant named Roger, a
Norman who had been with him for twenty years. He sent
Roger to visit all the lodging-houses where pilgrims stayed,
promising him a huge reward if he could find the King. It
did not take Roger long to identify the speech and figure of
the great Plantagenet. But neither the promised reward nor
his loyalty to his master could outbalance his feeling for the
man who was King of England and Duke of his own native
Normandy. With tears in his eyes he told Richard that
he would never betray him. He must escape at once. Roger
gave him a fresh horse, and went back to his master, saying
that the rumour was false that Richard was in the town.

Meanwhile, with only two companions, one a youth who
could speak German, Richard slipped away. For three days
and nights they pushed on as fast as their beasts could carry
them. At last, exhausted and famished, they were forced to
call at an inn near Vienna. They had no small change with
which to pay, but only some gold bezants, coins worth
between ten and twenty shillings and in modern money
vastly more. The youth was sent into Vienna to get change,
and suspicions were aroused. On a second journey he was
silly enough to carry his master's fine gloves thrust into his
belt. He was arrested and tortured until he admitted that his
master was indeed the English king. Richard's arch enemy,

Leopold, Duke of Austria, was himself in Vienna. He sent men to surround the inn. Richard said he would surrender his sword only to the Duke in person. Leopold hurried to the spot and had the immense satisfaction of receiving it. This happened a few days before Christmas, but that year, 1192, it was a cheerless Christmas for Richard, closely guarded in the remote mountain fortress of Dürnstein, over-looking the Danube. Guards watched him day and night with drawn swords, for the Lion-heart was already a legend of ferocity and they were taking no chances.

Richard was kept prisoner for just over a year, first by the Duke of Austria, later by the German Emperor Henry, who struck a bargain with the Duke. He was moved from one castle to another. Possibly to reduce the chances of a rescue-attempt, or possibly because news travelled so slowly, the authorities in England were for a long time kept in ignorance of his whereabouts. There is a story, which may or may not be true, that his friend, Blondel the minstrel, wandered from castle to castle, singing a song they had composed together, until an answering voice through the bars revealed that he had found the King. Certainly the official delegates sent out from England, the Abbot of Robertsbridge and the Abbot of Boxley, had to wander all over Western Germany and then only came upon him by good luck, as he was being moved from one prison to another. And it is equally certain that Richard, in his captivity, whiled away the time with minstrelsy, for we have a song he composed in both French and Provençal versions. One verse goes:

> "*Do the lads know, in Anjou and Touraine,*
> *Those lusty bachelors, those lively lords,*
> *That these foul walls their captive king constrain?*
> *Will they not bring me aid with loyal swords?*
> *Alas! no faith, no courage, now remain.*
> *Idle are sighs, and I must bear my chain.*"

During that year of Richard's captivity the news filtered through Christendom that his Saracen opponent, Saladin, had died of typhoid fever within a few months of the Crusaders' departure. It was a bitter thought for Richard. If only the French King had not left him, if only they had stayed a little longer . . . The Holy Land might by now have been theirs. But the only man capable of seizing it was kept, like a caged beast, by one who had been his comrade in the expedition.

Richard could not be rescued. He had to be ransomed, and England raised the immense sum demanded—150,000 marks —in record time. This says much for the efficient way in which his father had organised the government of the country. It says much too for Richard's popularity with the people whom he scarcely knew. Especially as John was plotting to have his brother kept prisoner for ever, and actually offering a cash sum to the Emperor for every month that he held Richard captive. Luckily their mother was still watching over the interests of her favourite son. The ancient Queen Eleanor knew her wily John, and was able to hinder his schemes.

At last Richard was released. He came back to England and went through a second ceremony of coronation at Winchester, as if to remove the stain of his captivity and to proclaim that he was home in all his glory as the King. But before this ceremony could take place he had to deal with various barons, supporters of John, who were in revolt against him.

Nottingham Castle was one of several great strongholds which refused to surrender until their defenders could be sure that Richard was really home. Envoys were sent out under a flag of truce. "What do you think?" he demanded. "*Am* I the King?" "Yes, sire." "Then go back, freely, as is right." The men returned to the castle, and the next day its garrison surrendered.

Richard spent the next day visiting Sherwood Forest, which

he had never seen before, and declared that it "pleased him well". In the old Robin Hood stories we hear how he came upon the outlaws and disclosed his identity to them, just as he had to the rebel envoys on the day before, and how Robin Hood knelt before him and was pardoned. There could well be truth in it. It depends mainly on whether our Robin Hood is the one mentioned in the official records of 1230 ("*Robertus Hood fugitivus*") who could have been alive at this time, or the one serving King Edward II in 1323, as some people think. But if Robin Hood *was* in Sherwood that day, it is very likely that he remembered how Richard had relaxed the forest laws and promised pardon to outlaws, in which case it would have been obvious common sense to stage a meeting as the royal party rode through the greenwood.

If there were troubles to settle in England, there were far more serious ones to attend to in his French domains. Five weeks after his visit to Sherwood, Richard took ship from Portsmouth. Though he lived for another five years, he never saw England again.

Those five years were spent in restoring his authority over his French vassals and in fighting King Philip, now his open enemy. He was hoping all the time that, once these troubles were over, he would be able to keep his vow and return to the Holy Land. It was during this period that he showed his genius as a castle-builder—and, incidentally, his ability to learn from his ingenious Saracen enemies—by raising the majestic stronghold of Château-Gaillard to defend his Norman boundaries against Philip. "How beautiful is my one-year-old daughter!" he exclaimed as he gazed upon the finished fortress after twelve months of toil.

He was never to have a daughter of flesh and blood. He had been rejoined by Berengaria—whatever trouble had arisen between them was smoothed away—but although she remained with him to the day of his death they never had any children.

His end came at the siege of Chalus, a paltry little fortress, involved in a trivial quarrel. Richard was wounded by a crossbowman, who, having lost his father and two brothers in wars against Richard, had waited patiently for the chance of revenge. The wound led to blood-poisoning, and on 6th April, 1199, with his mother and probably Berengaria also at his bedside, Richard's fierce heart ceased to beat. He was not yet forty-two—but in one sense he was ageless. For, as long as the tales of chivalry are told, he will have his place among the immortals.

THE YEARS BETWEEN 1199–1442

IN the two and a half centuries between the death of Richard I and the birth of Edward IV the Middle Ages pass from spring-time vigour to the rich fruitfulness (but also the decay) of autumn. With Edward we are near the end of the long Plantagenet pageant, almost in sight of the Tudor era, almost in sight of America.

In the meantime England has secured Magna Carta and, at least, the weak beginnings of a House of Commons. The great pestilence of 1348, later known as the Black Death, has wiped out between a half and a third of her population, and made deep changes in her life: after the plague almost every-thing, from the position of the working man to the style of cathedral architecture, is different. The first Edward has con-quered Wales and failed to conquer Scotland; the second has shown that a king can be deposed and murdered by his barons; the third has started the Hundred Years War with France, which has raged on, through Creçy and Poitiers to Henry V's Agincourt and Joan of Arc. The fourth Edward, as we shall see, is not without a distinction of his own.

His is a very different world from the Lion-heart's. Cathedrals and castles and costume look utterly changed. In peace, men wear fantastic fashions, with long pointed shoes and sack-like sleeves: in war, they have clapped on so much heavy plate-armour against the new gunpowder danger that, once knocked over, they cannot get up again.

4

Edward IV: The Rose of Rouen

HE was born at Rouen, and in later years, because he was handsome, men called him "the Rose of Rouen". In those days so flowery a nickname was not reserved for ladies only. It was fit for a fighter. At camp-fires, from deep and manly throats, the ballad would be heard:

> *"The Rose came to London, fully royally riding,*
> *Two archbishops of England they crowned the Rose king!*
> *Almighty Jesu save the Rose, and give him His blessing,*
> *And all the realm of England joy of his crowning."*

His mother, the lovely Cecily Neville, had been called "the Rose of Raby"—when she was not called "Proud Cis". His father, Richard Plantagenet, Duke of York, bore the White Rose emblem; there was a Red Rose of Lancaster; and in years to come the historians were to invent the name, "the Wars of the Roses", for the conflict between them. Thus, again and again, the symbol of the rose appears in Edward's story, but in no pleasant sense was it "roses, roses all the way". It was a life of dangerous adventure.

Edward was born at Rouen because his father was then governor of Normandy. The birth took place early on the morning of 28th April, 1442, in that same castle where Joan of Arc had been kept prisoner eleven years before. Edward was the third child of a family that went on growing yearly, but several of them died young, including his only elder brother, Henry. Edward was the eldest of the four boys who lived. The last of these, eight years younger than himself, was to go down in history and literature as Richard Crookback, King Richard III.

When they were born, however, no one could have foreseen that either boy would one day wear the crown.

Their father had certainly royal blood in his veins. He was descended from Edward III and, in strict logic, had perhaps a better claim to the throne than the ruling king, Henry VI, whose grandfather, Henry IV, had seized it from the childless Richard II. But all that was a long time ago. Henry VI had been unchallenged king since babyhood, and not even the Duke of York himself had ever suggested that the crown was on the wrong head.

All that was to come later.

Meanwhile, Edward's parents had great power and influence.

Not only had the Duke his own high family connections but his marriage to Cecily Neville had brought him inside a whole further network of useful relationships. The Nevilles were a numerous family—and an ambitious one. What titles and lands they did not hold by birth, they strained every nerve to get by marriage. As soon as Edward was old enough to tell one aunt or uncle from another, he realised that he was nephew to half the nobility.

Uncle Richard, by marrying the right heiress, had become Earl of Salisbury. Uncle William and Uncle Edward had so conveniently fallen in love that they blossomed forth as Lord Fauconberge and Lord Abergavenny respectively. Not to be outdone by their brothers, Aunt Katherine, Aunt Anne, and Aunt Eleanor had contrived to bestow their hearts on the Duke of Norfolk, the Duke of Buckingham, and the Earl of Northumberland. Uncle George, by way of variety, had won his title of Lord Latimer by succeeding his half-uncle. Uncle Robert had not married at all, and had contented himself with becoming a bishop—but a Bishop of Durham, which meant controlling a good deal of military power because of his nearness to the Scottish Border.

With uncles and aunts such as these (and all the men bound to follow their banners in war), a Neville family gathering was rather like the mobilisation of an army. If that is understood, it is easier to grasp why people acted as they did in a civil war, and, above all, how any particular lord chose which side to fight on.

But in the fourteen-forties young Edward, playing with his brother Edmund, only a year his junior, had no foreknowledge of the gathering storm.

Not much is known of Edward's childhood. He had a kind French nurse, Anne de Caux, and rewarded her kindness when he grew up. Probably he saw more of her, day by day, than of his beautiful mother, who, with her social responsibilities and her series of babies, had little time to spend with the older children. As for his father, the Duke of York was often away on public business. With a weak king on the throne, there was all the more for his nearest councillors to do.

When Edward was ten or eleven, he and Edmund were given their own household. Edward bore the title of the Earl of March and his brother was the Earl of Rutland. They lived in the splendid castle of Ludlow, in Shropshire. It was their father's home, but too distant from London for him to spend much time there. The great fortress stood on a rocky hill, girdled by the River Teme. From its high Norman keep they could see the wild mountain horizon of Wales.

Earls they might be, and their parents far away, but the two small boys were not at all free to do as they liked. Richard Croft, a Herefordshire gentleman of old family, supervised their lessons, and his wife looked after their general welfare. Croft was firm, firmer than the boys liked. They wrote to their father, complaining of "*the odious rule and demeaning of*

Richard Croft", but they got no more support than most other children find when they complain at home about their school. The Duke told them to work harder. At twelve years Edward was writing to him: "*. . . and where you command us to attend specially to our learning in our young age that should cause us to grow to honour and worship in our old age. Please it your Highness to wit that we have attended our learning since we came hither, and shall hereafter*."

Education was no longer something only for priests: as in Alfred's day, it was sought by others, rich or poor. The young king had founded Eton College only a few years before. England was already feeling, from a distance, the rising breeze of the Renaissance, the New Learning in Italy which was to blow away so many medieval cobwebs. However Edward might grumble against Croft's discipline (and in later years Croft too was remembered gratefully and rewarded), the young earl loved both reading and writing. Nor was education entirely bookish: he practised all the outdoor sports, notably riding, hunting, and the use of arms. He loved dancing and he had well-polished manners. Early in life he learnt to charm people of all classes, high and low, especially those of the opposite sex. He could talk clothes and fashions with them, just as he could talk business with the London merchants and soldiering with the finest generals of the age.

It was a keen, many-sided brain that developed under Croft's stern tutorship.

There were breaks in the routine, of course—long rides across England to stay at Fotheringay, another family-home, and visits to London. There were relations to meet, including the King and Queen.

Henry VI was by now in his early thirties, but he had been king ever since he could remember. He was a gentle, religious man, without any magnificence—he wore drab, unfashionable clothes and was said to dress like a farmer.

Though his father had been the fire-eating Henry of Agincourt, he himself was timid and utterly unwarlike. To a boy like Edward, athletic and full of life, the King was not an inspiring figure. The young earl soon realised, from the talk of noblemen and servants alike, that Henry was loved and pitied, but never feared or admired. It was whispered that he had inherited the taint of "midsummer madness" from his French grandfather, and that he was not merely weak of will but also weak in the head. There were jokes about his extreme modesty—how, at some Christmas entertainment, the girl-dancers had so shocked him by their low-cut dresses that he had rushed from the hall, and how, at Bath, he had been upset even to see men undressing to bathe in the hot springs.

The Queen, Margaret of Anjou, was very different. She had a southern temperament, all fire and storm, with the courage and obstinate will-power that her husband lacked. She had little tact in handling Englishmen. In one way it would have been better if she and her husband could have exchanged sexes; but, though Henry would have made a sweet and virtuous queen, Margaret might have been less successful as a king. Obstinacy was not enough. Englishmen had to be led, not driven, and, in the fifty years that the House of Lancaster had ruled, Parliament had been allowed to increase its powers.

The real rulers of England at this moment were whichever clique of noblemen could persuade Henry to do what they wanted. Edward's father, as a Plantagenet, kinsman of the King, and Duke of York, was a natural choice as right-hand man and adviser. His friends and followers—including his wife's far-spreading Neville connections—formed one party in the state. Another was formed, inevitably, by the other great families who disagreed with their policy or were jealous of their position.

Jealousy counted for more than disagreement. Politics

were still very personal. It was not a question of voting for new laws as in a modern democracy but of scheming (and if need be fighting) to get estates and offices.

When Edward was eleven, the King had a long spell of insanity. The struggle for power brought the rival barons almost to open civil war, but it was just avoided. Shortly before Edward's twelfth birthday came the good news that his father had been appointed Protector, to govern on behalf of the mad king.

Until a few months earlier, the Duke of York had been more and more hopeful that one day he might actually be king. Henry and Margaret had been married a long time without having any children and the prospect of seeing the meek and shy monarch as a proud father had become more and more unlikely. Soon the situation would have had to be faced and an heir chosen. With his descent from Edward III, the Duke was an obvious choice.

This hope faded with the birth, at last, of a prince. He too was baptised Edward, so, to avoid confusion, he may be called by his title, the Prince of Wales.

The other Edward, Earl of March, was quite old enough by now to understand how his own future might be affected by the arrival of this new distant cousin.

When the King recovered from his breakdown, after eighteen months, the Duke of York had to give up his post as Protector. His chief rival, the Duke of Somerset, came back into power: the Queen favoured him, and had no love for the Yorkists. As things were, to be out of favour could quite easily mean being *in* prison, or even out of this world. The rival parties mustered their forces. The threatened civil war broke out, which was to last off and on, with long intervals of quiet, for the next thirty years.

The Duke of York gathered most of his men from his estates in the north. Over in the west, at Ludlow, the thirteen-year-old Edward received the exciting summons to join his father with all the troops available there. The Duke of Somerset would be marching out of London to attack them.

It was May. Edward rode across the Midlands at the head of his little column of a few hundred men. They were mostly bowmen and billmen, the latter carrying pikes, axes, and other weapons. And there were a few knights in the immensely heavy plate armour of the fifteenth century, with long two-handed swords. The day of the cavalry charge was over, for the time being—even the knights dismounted before a battle began. In this campaign neither side had any artillery or hand-guns.

Edward joined his father. Their combined army numbered about three thousand. The Duke of Somerset was coming against them with a slightly smaller force. But *he* had a bigger proportion of noblemen with him, and he had the King as a sort of living figurehead. Through the King's mouth the Yorkists could be denounced as traitors and threatened with being hanged, drawn, and quartered. York's respectful message to Henry, explaining his actions, had been quietly pocketed by Somerset before it reached the King.

The two armies clashed in the narrow streets of St. Albans, just north of London. For a time they struggled hand to hand, neither side able to push back the other. Then there was a sudden blast of trumpets and the war-cry from an unexpected quarter: "A Warwick! A Warwick!" Edward's cousin, the Earl of Warwick, a thrustful young fighter of twenty-five, had found an unguarded route through the rabbit-warren of alleys and lanes which formed a medieval town. He gathered a band of his men inside some houses behind the enemy's lines, and then, breaking holes in the flimsy cottage-walls, burst out upon the Duke of Somerset's rear.

The struggle became more and more bloody. We have an eyewitness account from the pen of the old Abbot, John

Whethamstede, who was watching from the top of the abbey gateway. *"Here you saw one fall with his brains dashed out, there another with a broken arm, a third with a cut throat, and a fourth with a pierced chest, and the whole street was full of dead corpses."* Edward may not have been in the thick of it, but he must have seen plenty of horrors that morning. At the finish, the Duke of Somerset lay dead on the steps of the Castle Inn, the King (accidentally wounded in the neck by an arrow) had been taken into the house of a tanner to receive first aid, and the victorious Yorkist leaders had followed him there to kneel and, in theory, be "forgiven". They had not been fighting the King, they said, only his evil advisers. . . . But even Henry himself had the wit to see the real position, behind the mask of politeness.

The Duke of Somerset was dead, but the Queen lived, and she was the permanent enemy of the Yorkists, an ever-looming danger. The next few years were uneasy, and Edward, passing through his 'teens, understood more and more of what was happening.

King Henry had another mental breakdown, the Duke of York became Protector again, but Henry recovered more quickly this time and the Duke's power dropped low. It was like a perpetual seesaw, up and down. Now that Queen Margaret was on top, the Yorkists found it safer to keep away from court. The Earl of Warwick went back to Calais, the last corner of France held by England, where he commanded the garrison. The Duke of York retired to his castles on the Welsh Marches, dividing his time between Ludlow and the near-by castle of Wigmore in Herefordshire. In the hopes of getting rid of him, the Queen made Henry appoint him governor of Ireland, but the Duke calmly ignored the compliment and stayed where he was. The Queen was unpopular. Sooner or later she would go too far. If the Duke won another victory like that of St. Albans, he would take good care not to lose the advantage of it again.

One of the lessons young Edward had to learn was that you could be strong today and win a battle, yet weak tomorrow without having lost another. England was not neatly divided into two sides. There was a solid core of loyal friends, yes, and a gang of implacable enemies ranged against them. But the vast majority of Englishmen were neither Yorkist nor Lancastrian, and they would go streaming across from one side to the other for all manner of reasons.

He had his first sharp lesson when he was seventeen.

Queen Margaret made up her mind to crush the Yorkist party. Her strong will overcame not only Henry but the neutral members of his council. She raised a large army in the King's name and advanced into the Welsh Marches. The Duke knew he must fight or run. He would get no mercy from Margaret. The royal army was much larger than any he could raise, even there in the midst of his own people, but he decided to make a stand in front of Ludlow. The Earl of Warwick came hurrying over from Calais to help him, bringing a band of retainers in the familiar red jackets with the badge of a ragged staff upon them. Edward was glad to see them. His father's other friends were coming in slowly and in small numbers. Few liked the notion of open defiance to the King.

In earlier centuries the Duke of York might have defied his enemies from the battlements of Ludlow Castle, but gunpowder was putting an end to the old-time sieges, and tactics had become more open. So, as the royal army closed in upon him, the Duke took up a position at Ludford, just outside the town. It was mid-October and the autumn rains had flooded the river-meadows beside the Teme, which protected the Yorkists on one side. There was a big ditch, too, and they made a strong barricade with farm-carts and stakes.

Night came. The enemy had halted and encamped opposite the Yorkists. There was a night alarm—suddenly the primitive, iron-hooped cannon of the defenders began to

boom and flash in the darkness—but the expected attack did
not follow. Daylight brought more serious developments.
Some of the Duke's allies had deserted and gone over to the
King's camp under cover of dark. Already heavily outnumbered, the Duke saw his little army melting like a snowball.
The leaders held a hasty conference. They could sell their
lives dearly but uselessly—or live to fight another day. The
Duke explained to Edward that they had better separate. He
himself, taking Edmund, would ride into the Welsh hills, and,
if need be, cross to Ireland. Edward, as his heir, must take
another escape-route. The Earl of Warwick was making for
Calais, whence he could defy the Queen across the Channel.
Edward should go with him. His mother and two little
brothers, George and Richard, must stay in Ludlow Castle.
Even the Lancastrians would not harm innocent women and
children.

There was not a moment to waste. Edward galloped off
with Warwick and Warwick's father, the Earl of Salisbury,
Sir John Dynham, and two attendants. Their enemies were
in hot pursuit. The little party rode hard through Herefordshire and Gloucestershire, crossed the Severn, and swung
south-westwards down into Somerset and Devon. Somehow, somewhere, they must find a ship to take them to
France. The whole country was up behind them. They were
proclaimed traitors, with every man's hand against them.

They were near Barnstaple before they found a craft. Sir
John Dynham, being less likely to be recognised, went off and
managed to buy a fishing-boat for two hundred and twenty
nobles, about seventy pounds. A skipper and four hands were
signed on, officially to take the gentlemen to Bristol, but,
once they were safely out of harbour, Warwick surprised
them by asking if they knew the way in the opposite direction
—westwards, and round the perilous corner at Land's End.
No, they answered, not one of them had ever sailed in those
waters.

It was an ugly moment. The little group of weary fugitives faced the staring, suspicious seamen. Queen Margaret's vengeance was hot upon their heels. They were, indeed, between the devil and the deep blue sea. It was Warwick again who saved the situation.

"Please God and my lord St. George," he cried, stripping off his cloak and seizing the helm, "*I* will bring you to a safe harbour!"

He kept his word. Their adventurous gallop was followed by an equally exciting voyage. Warwick brought them safely past Land's End to Guernsey in the Channel Isles. There they were weather-bound for over a week, but at last the wind changed and they went scudding up the Channel to Calais on the wings of a storm.

What welcome awaited them? There had been time for the Queen to take action against Calais. Would Warwick's men have surrendered the town to her? As the weather-beaten vessel neared harbour, Edward wondered what would happen when they set foot ashore.

All was well. Calais was still held for the Yorkist party. Edward slept in a clean and comfortable bed that night, safe for the moment—but an exile and an outlaw.

His father meanwhile had reached Ireland, where, in the following March, the Earl of Warwick paid him a visit to discuss the next move. Edward stayed at Calais and, except while Warwick was in Ireland, was constantly with his warlike cousin. The Earl was a cousin any youth would have been proud to look up to. His example had a great influence upon the future king, not entirely for good. Warwick was too impatient of advice, too much of a dictator in his temperament.

Queen Margaret failed in her attempts to get possession of Calais, and when summer came the exiles struck back. The Duke published a manifesto from Ireland, listing all the

misdeeds of the King's advisers. The English people, with
their usual easy sympathy for the under-dog and their natural
dislike of any government, were all in favour of bringing back
the exiles. Edward and Warwick crossed the Channel with
two thousand men. Edward had his first heart-warming
experience of a great public welcome. Riding through the
Kentish villages in the June sunshine, he was cheered to
the echo. On the gates of Canterbury someone had hung
the ballad that many were singing—there was a reference to
himself in it:

> *"Edward, the Earl of March, whose fame the earth shall
> spread . . ."*

It was thrilling to be named in the same verse—

> *"With that noble knight and flower of manhood,
> Richard, Earl of Warwick, shield of our defence . . ."*

The Archbishop welcomed them at Sandwich. They rode
on, gathering supporters at every mile. The King and Queen
were not in London, they were hurriedly scraping together
an army at Northampton. Margaret had not been ready for
this. Edward and his cousin rode over London Bridge and
entered the capital without striking a blow. Their men
marched in between cheering masses of the townsmen, for
the city always favoured the Yorkist cause.

A week later they met the King's army at Northampton.
This time Edward was no boy, held back in comparative
safety, but commander of the advance guard, which became
the right-hand division of the three formed for the actual
assault on the King's camp. It was not a very bloodthirsty
business, for the Lancastrian rank-and-file had no heart in it.
Some broke and fled as Edward charged their trenches.
Others, throwing down their weapons, put out their hands

to help the Yorkists scramble up the muddy banks. This time it was the Queen who fled to Wales—and the King again was taken prisoner in the most respectful possible way.

Back in London, Edward had a happy reunion with his family. First his mother arrived with the younger children, George and Richard and his sister Margaret; they had been staying with their aunt, the Duchess of Buckingham, but the Lancastrians had kept a sharp eye on them and their situation had been awkward and anxious. Then, after a week or two, came the Duke himself from Ireland, with Edmund.

Edward found his father in a determined mood. He was not going to lose the fruits of victory a second time. He claimed nothing less than the crown, and presented Parliament with a long written statement, tracing his royal descent. If the King's grandfather, Henry IV, had really usurped the throne, it followed that neither Henry V nor Henry VI had been rightfully crowned. But Parliament remembered that it had been an earlier Parliament which had called Henry IV to the throne, and the members were unwilling to admit that all the actions of the past sixty years rested on a false foundation. Also, they were sorry for Henry VI and fond of him. They rejected the Duke's claim.

The Duke was furious—but his friends were no less angry that he had damaged their party by asking for too much. Warwick was always a good judge of public opinion. He did not mince words.

Young Edmund broke in to defend his father. "Fair sir, be not angry," he told his cousin, "for you know that we have the true right to the crown, and that my lord and father here must have it."

Edward was on Warwick's side. But all he said was, soothingly: "Brother, vex no man, for all shall be well."

Warwick stormed out of the room without a word of farewell to anyone but Edward. Later, when none of the other nobles could persuade the Duke to drop his claim, it was Edward who went to his father and persuaded him to see reason. A bargain was struck with Parliament. Henry was to remain King for life, but the Duke was to be heir apparent, instead of the little Prince of Wales, and the Duke's heirs were to inherit the crown after him.

The day after this settlement, Henry went in solemn procession to a thanksgiving service in St. Paul's. Edward walked slowly up the aisle behind him, his strong young fingers holding up the King's magnificent train. Henry was not a small man, but the handsome train-bearer overtopped him by a good six inches. Edward was eighteen and a half now, athletic and graceful, a Plantagenet to his finger-tips.

What thoughts passed through his head as they moved solemnly towards the altar, the November gloom of the cathedral lit up by the myriad candles lighted for All Saints Day?

His father seemed to have settled his destiny for him. The claim had been none of his, the family-feud was only something he had inherited, but now, by yesterday's agreement, his whole future was changed. Someday *he* would wear this crown, some day it would be his shoulders, not his hands, that would feel the weight of this royal train.

They had reckoned without the Queen.

Edward was just enjoying the new delights of London life —so pleasant to his taste after the quiet country existence at Ludlow and the hardships of exile and escape—still basking in new-heaped honours as Constable of Bristol Castle, Keeper of Kingswood Forest, and other West Country offices, when news came that the Queen was stirring in the north.

This time it was she, in theory, who was the rebel. Edward's father held Henry, and Henry must sign and seal documents accordingly. One of the commissions he granted was to Edward, to raise troops on the Welsh Marches against the Queen. Having collected them, he was to join his father and

Edmund, who had marched straight to the north, raising another army as they went.

It was December now. Edward stayed in Gloucester over Christmas, where there was good cheer at the great abbey which had so often entertained royal visitors. Then he rode up through the familiar counties which he had last seen as a hunted fugitive. He passed Ludlow and went on to Shrewsbury. There, terrible news met him.

His father had kept Christmas at Sandal Castle, just outside Wakefield, in Yorkshire. The enemy had surprised him. The Duke had been taken prisoner, given a mockery of a trial, and beheaded. Edmund had been killed as he tried to escape across Wakefield bridge. Later dispatches only piled on the horror. At the Queen's own orders, the Duke's head had been exhibited on the battlements of York city, wearing a paper crown. Edmund's head was another in the row, and so was that of Warwick's father, the Earl of Salisbury.

The civil war had entered a new phase. Rage and bitterness seized the Yorkists. Henceforth there would not only be battles but butcheries. Edward himself was never quite the same person again.

Almost at once he had to fight for himself—the first time he had been the general, without Warwick to lead the way. At Mortimer's Cross, a few miles from Ludlow, he met a force of foreign mercenaries, Frenchmen and Bretons and Irishman, led by two Lancastrian earls. Edward was in his own countryside. His boyhood rides had taught him every inch of this ground. It was a hazy February morning, the sky playing strange optical tricks with the sun and making it appear as three. (He afterwards added a sun to his white rose badge. A similar phenomenon was reported just after these lines were written—at Bridlington, Yorkshire, on 2nd March, 1954.) Edward met the enemy marching up the old Roman road, and crushingly defeated them. The most important prisoners were promptly beheaded. With the fate

of his father and brother still raw in his memory, he was in no
mood for mercy.

How much longer would his own head be on his shoulders?
The Queen was preparing to march south upon London.
Her rough northern troops were murdering and looting as
they advanced into the more prosperous areas. The news got
worse. There had been a second Battle of St. Albans—and
this time the invincible Warwick himself had been beaten.
The King had escaped—if you could call it escape. He was
now in the strong and capable hands of his wife. A warrant
was out for Edward's arrest. His mother had sent the two
younger boys abroad to Burgundy.

One thing alone favoured Edward. London loved him.
London, and all the south, feared the Queen's barbarian
northerners. The city sent him an urgent appeal to return
and protect it. Edward was already half-way there when the
Earl of Warwick met him in the Cotswolds and supported
the appeal.

Warwick said what was in many men's thoughts. The
Lancastrians had broken their side of the bargain over the
crown. The Yorkists were now free to act as they thought
best.

"You are already Duke of York, by your father's death,"
he pointed out to his young cousin. "Therefore, by strict
right, you should be King now, not merely after Henry's
death."

What neither Warwick nor the rest would have granted to
Edward's father a few months before, they were now quite
ready to grant Edward. "*Let us walk in a new vineyard, and let
us make a gay garden in the month of March,*" wrote one Yorkist
supporter, "*with this fair white rose and herb, the Earl of March.*"

When Edward rode into London, he was received tumultu-
ously. Even the welcome of the previous summer had been
as nothing compared with this. He came now as a deliverer.

He took up his lodging not in the Tower but in Baynard's

Castle, a fortress which then stood beside the Thames near
St. Paul's. Parliament was not in session, so, on the following Sunday, a big public rally was organised by Warwick and
the questions were put: Was King Henry worthy to reign
any longer? Would they have the Earl of March as king in
his place? The crowd voted "No" and "Yes" as they were
intended to, and a delegation was appointed to call upon
Edward. Tactfully, he did not agree at once. He hesitated,
so that the Archbishop of Canterbury and various noblemen
had to use persuasion. But in a day or two everything was
settled. The heralds proclaimed him, and, after a service at
St. Paul's, he went in state to Westminster. There he walked
to the throne, set in the Great Hall, and sat down on it, and
was acclaimed King. Other ceremonies followed in the
Abbey, and he took the royal oaths and received homage
from the barons, but the full coronation was postponed.

"I will not be crowned," Edward told them, "until I have
killed my father's enemies or driven them out of the country."

Before that month of March was out, he had gone a long
way towards doing so.

Edward met his father's enemies at Towton, ten miles
south-west of York, where Queen Margaret had retired to
re-organise her forces after her victories at Wakefield and
St. Albans. What a fool she had been, Edward must have
thought, not to push on and take London when she had been
so near! But the Londoners had closed their gates against her,
and she had turned back. She had missed her chance, perhaps
for ever.

Not that the coming battle was going to be easy for himse
Margaret had mustered every available man. He guessed that
her army contained about forty thousand. He could not
match that number—quite. He reckoned he had thirty-six
thousand. Never in history had such large armies clashed on
an English battlefield. Never (if Edward had known it) were

E

such numbers to be equalled again. And never was there to be a more horrid slaughter than on that Palm Sunday in 1461. The day dawned gloomily, with a keen south wind blowing against the enemy. By eleven o'clock it was beginning to snow. One of Edward's uncles, Lord Fauconberge, commanded the leading Yorkist division. Cunningly, he sent forward his archers to shoot a single volley, and then drop back. The Lancastrians, their eyes screwed up against the sleety wind, shot wildly in return, not one arrow each but most of their ammunition. They did not realise that their shafts, aimed into the wind, were falling fifty or sixty yards short of the target. When the shooting slackened, Fauconberge's men ran lightly forward and gathered up most of the arrows, leaving the rest stuck in the ground to hinder the enemy when they charged.

That charge soon came. The Lancastrian masses rolled down into the dip between the armies and mounted the slope on which Edward had drawn up his forces. The Yorkist bowmen let fly, shaft after shaft. The enemy came on. When they were really close, the bowmen stepped back through the gaps left for them, and the billmen closed their ranks. The hand-to-hand struggle began.

It raged for the rest of that wintry day. Weighed down by their armour, wielding massive weapons, no troops could have carried on so long without a breathing-space. Such pauses there were, from time to time, and Edward used them to feed his front line with fresh men. The enemy were doing the same.

All through the afternoon they hacked and hewed, until sometimes, in places, the dead and dying formed a barricade between them. Despite that first advantage scored by the Yorkist archers, the Lancastrians looked like pushing through their enemy's line. Edward fought on grimly, forbidding his men to give mercy or to ask it. He was expecting reinforcements. As the daylight waned, these new troops came streaming up in bands. Gradually he was able to build up his right flank, deepen it and extend it to enfold the end of the line opposite. The Lancastrians began to falter and lose heart. Neither Henry nor Margaret was there to rally them: the nineteen-year-old Edward was pitted against a general little older than himself, the twenty-four-year-old Duke of Somerset. Suddenly the Lancastrian front wilted and the first fugitives began to dribble away. Panic followed. The routed soldiers all made for the one ford across a small but swollen river which barred their escape. The Yorkists pressed behind them, cutting them down. Men spoke afterwards, shuddering, of a bend in the river where the bodies had piled up into a dam, a causeway of the dead, over which the living trod a frightful path to safety.

No one ever numbered exactly the casualties that day. Perhaps twenty thousand Lancastrian dead, and the other half of their army finished as a military force—scattered, like the snow-flakes, on that cruel blast from the south. The King, the Queen, and the little Prince of Wales were in flight for Scotland, with their defeated general not far behind.

Edward lost about twelve thousand men, but hardly any nobles. This time, it had been the day of the common man.

He rode into York in triumph. At last he was able to take down the heads of his father and brother from Micklegate Bar, and give them honourable burial. Fresh heads replaced them. The mood, for the present, was revenge.

Now there could be talk of coronations. He was King of England in fact as well as in name.

Edward had shown himself a good general, in spite of his youth—but he had yet to show himself a ruler. He had not the single-minded greatness of Alfred or William the Conqueror. He was a very human young man, and, like most people, he kept a zigzag course between duty and pleasure. He loved banquets and tournaments. He delighted in music, and appointed a new band of royal minstrels. He liked the best in furniture and clothes. He flirted shamelessly with pretty women, and cared little if they were already married. Standards of conduct were not so strict in the fifteenth century—especially kings' conduct—but even so there were plenty of people who criticised him as self-indulgent and immoral.

He had his conscientious side, too, when he turned to public business with energy and intelligence. He had a great respect for justice. He liked to see things and learn for himself. He sat on the King's Bench beside his own Chancellor to hear cases tried. He travelled long distances through almost every part of his kingdom—his "royal progresses" covered far more ground than those of Elizabeth I in her far longer reign. He established the first postal system, with relays of horsemen every twenty miles to the Scottish Border.

He was keenly interested in trade, which was becoming more and more important to England. He was at ease with the merchants of London and Bristol, and not too proud to trade on his own account. He chartered ships, loaded them with English wool, cloth, and tin, and sent them to Greece and Italy. With these profits, and other devices, he managed to run the country without much dependence on Parliament and taxes. The English liked a king who tried to live on his own income.

Edward could be as revengeful and bloodthirsty as any other leader of his period. Sometimes. But not always. Often he was gentle and forgiving. He preferred to pardon when he could. In the course of the struggle he ordered some cold-blooded executions—that was the manner of the age. In this century no less than four English kings and twelve princes—not to mention countless noblemen—met violent ends. But at other times he was generous with pardons and set prisoners free without ransom.

He grew up into kingship gradually. For the first three years after Towton and the coronation festivities which followed, he felt a natural reaction. He was young. He wanted to enjoy himself after all he had gone through. And Cousin Warwick, his old hero, was at his side, full of experience and energy, only too willing to relieve him of his duties.

"*They tell me that they have but two rulers in England,*" a Frenchman reported ironically to Louis XI in Paris, "*Monsieur de Warwick, and another, whose name I have forgotten.*"

When Edward was twenty-one he met Elizabeth Woodville, the daughter of Lord Rivers. She was a little older than he, a beautiful young widow with two small sons. It was said that they first met romantically, when he was hunting in Wychwood Forest. Very soon, he was madly in love with her.

His mother told him they could not possibly marry. He ought to marry a princess, not a subject who had been one of Queen Margaret's ladies-in-waiting. Warwick, in particular, would be furious with him.

Edward decided to go his own way. On May Morning he rode off early, saying he intended to go hunting with Lord Rivers. Instead, he galloped straight to Elizabeth's home at Grafton, married her secretly, with her mother and one or two other people as witnesses, and returned to his court that evening alone, without telling anyone. Bride and bridegroom managed to steal a few more hours together during the four days following. Then, as the court was moving on, they had to say good-bye for a while.

It was not until September that the secret was revealed. The Privy Council, meeting at Reading, begged the King "in God's name to be wedded and to live under the law of God and the Church". Edward said he was quite willing, but was afraid they might not approve of his choice. What about Elizabeth Woodville? There was a chorus of objections. With a smile Edward remarked that it was a little late to object: they had been married since the first of May.

As he had been warned, Warwick was furious. The rift in their friendship dated from then.

Warwick was a true Neville—the most ambitious and arrogant of that whole thrustful family. He felt that it was he who had made Edward what he was. He had overlooked the fact that all pupils grow up and go their own ways. He had hoped to continue managing Edward and England indefinitely.

There was no love lost between the Nevilles and the Woodvilles. Elizabeth's family could be just as thrustful in their own interests. The lovely bride was herself no Juliet, despite her romantic wooing. She was a cool-headed schemer. It was no chance that she had met Edward in Wychwood Forest that first time. She too had been hunting, when Edward rode across her path. . . .

The marriage itself proved reasonably happy. They had a number of children, including those famous "Princes in the Tower" whose later murder became one of the unsolved crimes of history. (If their uncle, Richard III, was not the murderer, was it the cunning usurper, Henry VII?) But if Elizabeth made an average wife, she was less successful as a queen. She wheedled Edward to favour her relatives, and lost him much of his popularity with the upper class.

And all the time the Red Queen, Margaret, was tirelessly plotting to checkmate the White King, Edward. It mattered little that her husband was a prisoner again: after hiding for a long time with friends in the Lake District, poor Henry had been betrayed and captured in Lancashire. Edward had lodged him in the Tower. But Margaret knew that in this particular chess-game Henry was not really the Red King, but only a pawn. The struggle could go on very well, whether or not he remained on the board. She bided her time.

Meanwhile, Warwick played a game of his own. Edward

himself was surprised at a country manor and made prisoner. Now, England had two captive kings. Warwick tried to rule with Edward as his puppet. He soon found that Edward did not answer to the pull of the strings as Henry would have done. Edward broke free and Warwick fled abroad. There he struck a bargain with Queen Margaret, changed sides, and invaded England with an army, to release Henry and restore him to the throne. Not for nothing was Warwick nicknamed "the King-maker".

Again Edward was taken by surprise—but he had some excuse, for he could hardly have foreseen that his own brother George, Duke of Clarence, would desert to the enemy. He was asleep in bed at Doncaster when the serjeant of minstrels roused him with the news that a hostile party was within half an hour's ride and intended to capture him. The road to London was barred. The only escape-route was across the dangerous sands of the Wash. Edward leapt into the saddle and rode for the sea.

Once again he was fleeing for his life. Strange to think that it had been *with* Warwick, before—and now it was *from* Warwick and his allies! It was a nightmare ride. Several of his companions were drowned when the tide came racing in across the sandy levels. Edward himself had a narrow escape. At last he reached Bishop's Lynn, seized what shipping was available, and filled it with his men. The others he advised to make their peace with the Earl, while remembering that he himself was their king. He would return. He put to sea and ran for the Dutch coast. On the way, he was nearly captured by German privateers of the Hanseatic League, but he got safely ashore, so empty-handed, though, that he had to reward his ship's captain with a fur-lined gown instead of passage-money.

Queen Elizabeth and the children had been in London when the revolution took place. They found sanctuary in Westminster, and waited for rescue.

Edward spent this second spell of exile at The Hague and Bruges, where he got on well with the prosperous, cultured merchants of the Netherlands. He was organising and planning his counter-stroke against Warwick and Margaret. But plotting was not a full-time occupation. There were days of waiting for messengers—days when nothing further could be done until certain news arrived. With his usual zest for life, Edward did not mope during these interludes. He browsed happily in the private library of his host, the Seigneur de la Gruthuyse, whose collection of books was one of the finest in Europe. He went to see the new invention of printing, demonstrated by Caxton, who was later to move to London under his patronage. It was in Bruges that Edward really became a book-lover. Life before then had been rather too full of other matters.

There was no possibility of returning to England at the head of a big invasion force. He knew he must gamble on his own popularity—and the unpopularity of his enemies. Give Margaret and Warwick enough rope, and they would hang themselves. When he judged the time was ripe, he sailed.

He landed in Yorkshire, at that same Ravenspur where Henry IV had landed seventy years or so before, in his bid for the throne against Richard II. With grim amusement, Edward repeated—against his grandson, Henry VI—the very trick he had used: he pretended that he had returned, not to claim the throne, but only to ask for the family dukedom which was his by right. Again the trick worked. The local people did not resist him. He had time to gather strength. Only then did he throw off the mask and proclaim that he had come home as King.

Two battles followed. At Barnet, outside London, he met Warwick and utterly defeated him; when he heard that his one-time hero and friend was captured, he gave orders to spare his life, but he was too late—he found only Warwick's

Edward IV

body, stripped of its armour. Within the month, at Tewkes-bury in the West Midlands, he had crushed a second army raised by Margaret herself. In this battle died Margaret's son, the Prince of Wales. With him, and a great number of their supporters, died also the real hopes of Lancaster.

Henry VI died in the Tower a few weeks later. Officially he died of "pure displeasure and melancholy". More likely, he was murdered. It was not in line with Edward's character to approve such an action, but the temptation to settle every-thing for good and all must have been very strong. With Henry and his only son dead, with Margaret a harmless prisoner who could never bear another prince to claim the throne, there need be no more civil strife in England.

Whatever the truth of Henry's sudden death, there certainly was peace throughout the rest of Edward's reign. In many respects it was a golden period, like the last glory of the sunset, before medieval England gave place to the England of the Tudors.

Traces of that sunset glory linger in the architecture of Windsor Castle, where Edward built St. George's Chapel, and of the Divinity School at Oxford, with its exquisite roof, built at the same time. It lingers too in the illuminated manu-scripts and in the first printed books of Caxton, both of which Edward had learnt to appreciate during his stay in Bruges. It lingers in the prose of Sir Thomas Malory, depicting in his *Morte d'Arthur* the age of chivalry which was fast passing away.

Edward was virtually the last of the medieval kings—it is hardly worth counting the two-year interlude between his death and the arrival of the Tudors. But he was also half a modern. He looked forwards as well as back. The grand-fathers of the Elizabethan sea-dogs were beginning to explore the ocean sea-routes in Edward's time, and with his encourage-ment. In some ways he was less like his Plantagenet forbears and more like a prince of the Italian Renaissance—such as

Lorenzo the Magnificent, with whom he corresponded. With the old nobility slaughtered on a dozen battlefields within as many years, the White King was left in lonely possession of the board. Edward was more or less forced to become one of the new-style monarchs, a single-handed ruler, a dictator perhaps, but in his case an amiable, warm-hearted and well-meaning one, despite a host of human weaknesses.

He died on 9th April, 1483, after a brief illness. He was only forty, but he had packed a great deal—far too much, said some—into that short life. The Rose of Rouen was laid to rest in the new chapel at Windsor. Very soon, now, the white flower and the red were to be blended, at last, in the emblem of the Tudors.

THE YEARS BETWEEN 1483-1600

BETWEEN the last of the Plantagenets and the first of the Stuarts lies perhaps the most familiar period in English history—the sixteenth century, the age of Henry VIII and the first Elizabeth, of Drake and the Armada, of Cardinal Wolsey and Robert Cecil, Sir Thomas More, Sir Walter Raleigh, Shakespeare, Marlowe, and a host of other immortal names.

The civil strife of York and Lancaster becomes an old story, fit subject for chronicles and stage-plays. Only a few short-lived riots and brief hopeless rebellions disturb the peace of Tudor England. There are no battles worthy of the name. The old nobility, like Kilkenny cats, have fought each other to the point of extermination, and there is no one left strong enough to defy a king or queen. The battlemented castles have given place to mansions and manors. Other people live more and more comfortably in farms and cottages (one thinks at once of such familiar buildings as Shakespeare's birthplace at Stratford and Anne Hathaway's cottage near-by at Shottery) and many a village street is already taking on the look it still wears today.

England has had the Reformation and the dissolution of the monasteries: she has ceased to be a medieval, Roman Catholic country, she has become Protestant and (as historians use the word) "modern". Religion is a burning issue, mixed up with politics. Men are prepared to fight and die for it. Such a man is Charles Stuart, soon to take the stage.

5

Charles: The Sad Cavalier

H<small>E</small> was born in Scotland, spoke with a strong Scots accent all his life, and preferred Scotsmen around him to Englishmen. Yet it was his fate to see Scotland only once or twice after his babyhood, to lead his troops against a Scottish army, and at the last to be sold by Scotsmen to his English enemies.

Charles entered the world on the 19th November, 1600, at Dunfermline Castle near the Firth of Forth, sixteen miles from Edinburgh. Here, too, his father had been born before him—King James VI of Scotland, soon to be King James I of England. It was a spot famous in Scottish history. In the great abbey near-by lay such national heroes as Malcolm Canmore and Robert the Bruce.

His early memories of his parents were sketchy. He was a delicate child, and it was thought best to leave him in the country quiet of Dunfermline while they were holding court in their palace at Holyrood. He saw more of the doctors and nurses appointed to look after him, and of Lord Fife his official guardian. But, when his father did visit him, he was aware of a fattish man, whose clothing was so quilted and padded that he seemed even fatter, and so soft and yielding and puddingy to the childish embrace that it was sometimes hard to believe that there was a real man inside the cushioning. When the man bent to kiss his son, he was found to have a thin, straggly beard and wet lips. It was noticeable, too, that James washed even less—much less—than most people in that far from particular age.

Charles probably enjoyed his mother's kisses more. The Queen—Anne of Denmark—was a gay, feather-brained creature, with a passion for acting and dancing. What need for brains there? Had not her husband enough for both? But James was so solemn with his learning—was he not to go down in history as "the wisest fool in Christendom"? The little boy would not have been alone in his taste if he had preferred the laughing gaiety of the Scandinavian girl. He too, though, had a strong dash of his father's solemnity.

He had a brother, Henry, six years older, and a sister, Elizabeth, four years older than himself. Henry he must have admired and envied—everyone admired Henry, so healthy and good-looking and full of life. And his sister had all the same charm and high spirits. Charles's love for Elizabeth was the strongest emotion in his early life.

Soon after his second birthday, he lost—for the time being —these lively companions. He was too young to understand just why they had vanished from his daily life. The Queen of England, that wicked old woman who had once cut off the head of his grandmother, Mary Queen of Scots, had died at last. A gentleman, Sir Robert Carey, had galloped northwards at breakneck speed to offer James the sapphire ring he had snatched from the still-warm finger of the dead Elizabeth. It was a long-awaited sign. James had his plans made to take over his inheritance. He started south for England with his wife. Soon Henry and Elizabeth were sent for to join their parents. But it was thought that Charles, a sickly, backward child, unable either to walk or to talk properly, was better left in Scotland.

It was more than a year before (in July, 1604) the doctors said he was fit for the long journey. The little boy travelled in a closed litter. Over the appalling roads of the seventeenth century even an ordinary traveller took more than a week. It was probably longer than that before the litter halted in the courtyard of an inn at Northampton, the curtains were pulled back, and the little prince was lifted out on to the cobbles, where his father, whom he had almost forgotten, stood ready to meet him.

Poor Charles! No one, looking at that puny mannikin, stumbling both in walk and speech, could have foreseen that he would live to wear more royal dignity than almost any other British sovereign, before or after him.

"Mannikin" is a fair description, for, like all the children of the period, Charles was enveloped in heavy garments reaching to his ankles. There were no distinct children's clothes as we understand them. When he first arrived in England he was probably still wearing a full-length coat, hiding under-coats or "petticoats". But very soon, at about six, he would be solemnly "breeched"—fitted, that is, by the tailor with a complete adult suit in miniature, with coat and waistcoat (and if need be corsets to make them fit well), and even a plumed hat and tiny sword.

Henry was rather unkind about Charles's weak legs. When he was King himself, he said, he would make "Baby Charles" his Archbishop of Canterbury. Then the legs could always be hidden by flowing robes. As he said this, Henry picked up the Archbishop's hat (for the actual Archbishop was at that moment in the next room with their father), and clapped it on his brother's head. Charles was so furious that he flung the hat on the floor and stamped on it, and it was all Henry could do to rescue it in a fit state for its owner to wear again.

Charles's temper was understandable. He was always being made to feel inferior. Those wretched legs! His father had wanted to make him wear irons to strengthen them. His new governess had saved him from that misery. Lady Carey, wife of that Sir Robert Carey who had posted northwards with the sapphire ring, had taken over the care of Charles, and she flew to his defence like a hen with one chick. No irons, no operation on the tongue to cure his defective speech! James gave way. For the next seven years Charles lived under

Lady Carey's kindly wing, first in one of the King's country-houses near London, then in another.

Year by year he grew stronger. He never lost a slight hesitation in his speech, but it never hindered him in his public duties. He would never have the athletic grace of Henry, but at least he could move across a hall without his father's ungainly waddle. He could dance well enough, too.

When he was ten, he danced in a masque at court. It was called the *Masque of the Rivers* and had been specially written for the celebrations when Henry was created Prince of Wales.

Masques were what the Queen loved. The dances, the tableaux, the music, the lighting effects, could be enjoyed with less mental effort than the play. Even Shakespeare had taken note of the changed tastes and fashions at court: he had just included a masque in his latest comedy, *The Tempest*, and now would trouble to write no more.

The Queen herself took part in the *Masque of the Rivers*. She was Tethys, the sea-goddess, with a sea-shell helmet and a blue robe laced with silver seaweed. Elizabeth sat at her feet looking very lovely as the Nymph of the Thames. Charles himself was arrayed in a green tunic sprigged with flowers, and wore wings of silver gauze. He had an important part. First he had to lead a *corps-de-ballet* of twelve nobly-born little girls. Then he had to present his father, in the audience, with Neptune's golden trident and his brother with a jewelled sword and the scarf their mother had embroidered for the occasion.

Charles got through his part without mishap, and to great applause. His legs could not be so bad after all! But the feeling of inferiority was by now too deeply implanted for it to be removed by any success. All his life, Charles was happier in the saddle than on foot.

Riding! His eyes would kindle at the thought. On horseback he was equal to anyone, even Henry. Henry loved a good gallop but was not a really keen huntsman. Charles himself developed a life-long passion for the sport, and became in time one of the finest horsemen in the kingdom. Riding after his hounds, he knew none of the fears and doubts which haunted him at other times. Once, as a man, galloping through that New Forest which had already claimed one English king as victim, he plunged into a deep bog. The horse was drowned. Charles was not pulled out until the ooze was sucking at the lace about his throat. Yet no sooner was he safe than he demanded a change of clothes and a fresh mount, on which he thundered away in quest of the stag. In the saddle, Charles was a different person.

He had a wistful longing to shine as a man of action. Henry, of course, would be King of England one day: Charles did not grudge him that. Despite Henry's teasing, he grudged him nothing. Had he not once written to Henry: "*Sweet, sweet brother, I will give anything that I have to you, both my horse, and my books and my fowling-pieces, and my crossbows, or anything that you would have . . .*"? Yes, Henry would be King Henry IX of England. Elizabeth would be a German princess: her engagement would shortly be announced to Frederick, the Elector Palatine. But what would he himself become?

Certainly not Archbishop of Canterbury—sincere and devout though he was in his prayers! He wanted to be a soldier. Why not a soldier of fortune, serving some great foreign power such as the Republic of Venice? Many a man of noble blood had served under the Venetian flag, like Othello in Shakespeare's play. The pale Scots boy dreamed his own dream of

> "*battles, sieges, fortunes . . .*
> *Of moving accidents by flood and field;*
> *Of hair-breadth scapes i' th' imminent deadly breach;*
> *Of being taken by the insolent foe. . . .*"

Suddenly, two weeks before his twelfth birthday, the dream was shattered. For ever, it seemed to him. He was spared the foreknowledge that, in a terrible way, its fulfilment was only postponed.

London was buying fireworks and heaping up bonfires ready for Guy Fawkes Night. It was just seven years since the discovery of the Gunpowder Plot, which was to have blown up his father and Henry and both Houses of Parliament. And now Henry, who had escaped that death, was stricken with a mysterious fever. He lay delirious at a country house in Essex. Even his father was dissuaded by the doctors from entering the sick-room. He gave orders that no other member of the royal family should run the risk, but Elizabeth, with her usual spirit, disobeyed her father and went down to Essex in disguise, only to be recognised and turned away. On 6th November Henry, Prince of Wales, and darling of the English people, died. The pale, sad-eyed younger brother knew then that, if he lived long enough, it was he who must follow his father as King of England.

Charles knew what it meant to be a king. No son of James I could be in any doubt about it. Charles had heard his father on a great number of topics—on the wickedness of tobacco-smoking and the obstinacy of Puritans and the impertinence of Parliaments—but on no subject more eloquently than that of kingly rights. In a speech to Parliament, just before Henry's death, James had declaimed in his broad Scots accent: "The state of monarchy is the supreme thing upon earth. Kings are God's lieutenants upon earth and sit upon God's throne. As to dispute what God may do is blasphemy, so it is treason in subjects to dispute what a king may do in the height of his power. I will not be contented that my power be disputed on."

God's lieutenant . . . That was what he too must be. Never in his life did Charles budge from the teaching his father had laid down. A king could not be wrong. However humble and modest he might be as a private individual, a king must never yield an inch of ground to his subjects. That was his duty, not only to himself but to his successors on the throne, and to the divine power which had set him there.

Little did James guess that in laying down this dogma he was sharpening the axe for his own son's neck and opening up a road which would lead his grandson, James II, into hopeless exile.

Charles was lonelier after Henry's death. Elizabeth's engagement had been announced soon afterwards, and soon his adored sister departed overseas to begin her new life. Charles never saw her again. The royal family was now quite broken up. The King no longer cared for the Queen and seldom spent any time with her. He preferred the company of his young noblemen—especially the brilliant George Villiers, whom he was rapidly promoting through all the successive grades of the peerage. The Queen was often unwell. She could no longer shine like a sun in the middle of her court, but spent more and more time quietly in the country. Charles could not visit her as much as he would have wished. He had had to take over Henry's former home, St. James's Palace, for even a boy prince must have his separate household, and there he lived, a stone's throw from his father at Whitehall, with his own host of officers and attendants.

The court-life disgusted him, with its gambling and its immorality, its cruel gossip and its shameless self-seeking. He might have echoed the lines of Walter Raleigh—Raleigh, the prisoner in the Tower, who had been Henry's friend and hero, and was now soon to die as the victim of their father's meanness:

> *"Go tell the Court it glows*
> *And shines like rotten wood . . ."*

Charles turned from the uncleanness of Whitehall. He trained his body like a modern schoolboy, taking daily runs.

He insisted on mastering great chargers that were thought too strong and fiery for him. And he mastered them. He rode in the tilt-yard, for the old medieval tournaments still lingered as a picturesque survival. He played tennis.

He never grew tall. That was another reason why he felt more confident when he was on horseback. But he was good-looking—people said he took after his mother. His forehead was high, his hair lightish brown, his dark eyes certainly more thoughtful and melancholy than the Queen's. Later, a neat, pointed beard was to give an added length and sharpness to his face—or a foxiness, his enemies might say.

When he was sixteen, he was made Prince of Wales. He was glad that his father was sufficiently pleased with him to confer the title. He might not be *worthy* to follow poor Henry and wear the ostrich-plumes, but at least the King did not think him hopelessly unfit.

Charles was hungry for his father's approval and bitterly jealous of the young men like Villiers, now Marquis of Buckingham, so much more showy than himself, who had first claim on the King's company. He had several childish quarrels with Buckingham. Once, in the gardens of Green-wich Palace, he lay in wait for him where there was a water-spout concealed among the trees (a form of practical joke highly popular in the seventeenth century), and, suddenly turning on the tap, drenched his rival. James was so furious that he boxed his ears soundly for it. But Buckingham showed great tact and gradually won over the sulky boy. In time he became the closest friend—almost the only close friend—Charles ever had.

That friendship was soon to be needed. At eighteen Charles lost his mother. She died at Hampton Court. He hurried to her bedside, hardly realising how ill she was. His father, callous and indifferent, did not interrupt his hunting at Newmarket.

That was the year before the *Mayflower* sailed from

Plymouth, carrying Puritans who preferred the unknown perils of America to the Church of England discipline demanded by the King. Men were prepared to emigrate for freedom, but they did not yet think of fighting. . . .

Charles was twenty, twenty-one, twenty-two . . . He was shy and had so far shown little interest in girls, but it was time to think of a wife for him. There was talk of a French princess, but peace-loving James was more interested in strengthening friendship with the old enemy, Spain. The Spanish ambassador, Gondomar, was a typical grandee, haughty, cultured, superb. He charmed not only James, but Charles too. He dropped hints about a possible marriage with the Infanta of Spain. Charles was flattered and grew interested. Gondomar gave him the princess's colours, sent specially from Madrid, and Charles wore them on his helmet in the tilt-yard. But time passed, and the matter went no further, as Gondomar did not intend it to. He was merely using the suggestion as a decoy, to keep England friendly.

Charles and Buckingham—"Steenie", as the King called him—were not satisfied to let the matter drop. Why should they not go to Madrid, suggested Steenie, and woo this Spanish beauty? They could travel incognito, it would never do for them to go officially, but for that very reason it would be a delightful adventure. James heard of the idea, laughed, and forbade it, but if he did not take it seriously neither did the young men pay too much attention to his ban.

They went ahead with their plans in secret. One Monday in February they asked the King for two days' leave of absence from court to go hunting.

"See that you be with us on Friday night," said James.

"Sire," said Buckingham, "if we should stay a day or two longer, I hope your Majesty will pardon us?"

"Well, well," murmured James, and, probably guessing what was afoot, asked no more questions.

They set off with three or four attendants the next morning.

Charles and Steenie had donned false beards and muffled themselves in vast riding-coats. One of the beards fell off as they clattered through Gravesend. It was carried to the local mayor who, suspecting treason, sent an officer to overtake the mysterious strangers. Steenie dealt with the officer with his usual charm and skill, and sent him back with a promise to keep his mouth shut. Taking a roundabout route they made for Dover, where there were more awkward questions to answer before they could sail. They were both sick crossing the Channel, but at last they landed safely in France, and started post-haste for Paris. Steenie fell off four times on the way.

They stayed five days in Paris and wrote a reassuring letter to the King. Thus, by the time they reached Madrid, the news had gone ahead of them, and they were given a public welcome. The Spaniards were polite but they avoided any definite promises. Charles was not allowed to meet, or even to get a close view of, the princess he hoped to marry. This was not England, he was told, but Spain. The Infanta led a secluded life, like any other well-bred girl. Charles did not actually serenade her, but he tried other means of seeing what she was like. He climbed a tree so that he could look over her garden-wall and steal a glimpse of her, and, as the weeks passed without any clear progress, he had the best spy-glasses in London sent out to him, to focus upon her too-distant charms.

Meanwhile, in England, there was strong public feeling against the match. England wanted no Spanish queen. The summer passed. James was ill and wanted his son home. Steenie, who had left a young wife and child of his own behind, was tired of the Madrid adventure. It had gone far, far beyond a joke. . . . An English fleet was sent to bring the Prince of Wales home, with or without a bride, in a manner fitting to his rank. The Prince came home without—and the delight of the English people more than made up for the failure of his wooing. Charles was welcomed with bell-ringing and bonfires. He was dumbfounded to find himself for the first time in his life (and as it proved the last) a genuine popular hero. And all because he had come home without the girl.

Just over a year later, in the spring of 1625, James died. For a week Charles shut himself up in his apartments. When he came out, he looked paler than ever, and sadder, for despite all his father's faults, he had deeply loved the grotesque old king. In a long black cloak he walked across the park to Whitehall, henceforth to be the main setting of his life, and, had he but known it, his death.

"Charles, by the Grace of God, King. . . ."

The heralds' formula was no string of empty words to the new sovereign. Charles felt he *was* King by the grace of God. He was the Lord's anointed, "God's lieutenant", as his father had said to Parliament years before. His whole position rested on the divine right of kings.

In that spirit he began by cleaning up the life of the court. There was to be an end of the bad old ways, "the beastly delights" (as one witness termed them) which had shocked him as a child. There must be decency and order, respect for religion.

"If he will not come to my prayers," cried Charles, when one courtier avoided the daily service, "let him get out of my house!"

On the other hand, nobody was sent away from court if his conduct was satisfactory. It had been the normal practice for a new sovereign to dismiss the former officers and hand out their posts to his own favourites. Charles felt that this was unfair.

Whitehall was easy to control: Parliament was a different matter. When he opened his first Parliament at Oxford he received an unpleasant shock.

Hitherto, a new sovereign had been granted the revenues known as tunnage and poundage for the rest of his life. To Charles they were voted only for the coming year.

There were men in Parliament who did not share his belief in the divine right of kings. They believed that kings and peoples should work in partnership, both under the law, and that it was as wrong for the king to break that partnership as for his people to do so. But there was only one way to control him, and that was to keep a tight hold on the purse-strings.

If a king had money, he could govern indefinitely without troubling to call Parliament. Even the popular Elizabeth had avoided calling together her "faithful Commons" except when she was driven to it by want of money. In 1603 Parliament had made the mistake of voting tunnage and poundage to James for life. They did not mean to repeat their mistake in 1625. There was nothing personal against Charles in what they did. They were simply seizing a chance which, if he lived to a ripe old age, might not offer itself for another half-century.

But to Charles it was intensely personal. One of the first things for which he needed money was military aid to his sister's husband in Bohemia. It was a blow at his beloved sister as well as an insult to his royal dignity. He accepted the situation because he could do nothing else, but he noted his enemies and remembered them.

He had other things, too, to think of in those first months of his reign. It was a king's duty to marry and have children to inherit the throne. England had gone through enough doubt and anxiety under an unmarried queen and the child-less monarchs before her. Now he was King, Charles must settle the marriage question.

His bride was already chosen. She had been approved before his father's death. Now it was time to proceed with the wedding.

Charles was to marry Henrietta Maria, sister of the French king and daughter of the gay and dashing Henry of Navarre. If Charles had ever seen her—which was just possible, when he visited the French court incognito during his five-day visit to Paris—he had no distinct memory of her. She was a Roman Catholic, but his people were far more ready to accept a French princess of that religion than the Infanta of Spain. Besides, she was little more than a child, who could be moulded into a suitable Queen of England.

The marriage took place by proxy before she left Paris. Charles could not leave the country to fetch her, but the court moved down to Canterbury to await her arrival. When news came that she had landed at Dover, he mounted his horse impulsively and galloped over the Kentish Downs to welcome her.

He arrived unheralded, without ceremony, a pale young man of twenty-four in a plain riding-suit. At the best of times he was simple in his dress. After the resplendence of Elizabeth and the balloon-like bombast of his father's clothes, Charles made a dark, elegant figure, lit by small touches such as his silver cane, an occasional diamond, or the Mechlin lace at his collar.

Henrietta was changing. He had to wait. After a few minutes he saw her coming down the long hall towards him —a flushed, eager girl of fifteen. She knelt and kissed his hand. He raised her and kissed her over and over again. Then, at arm's length, they stared and smiled at each other. She was *petite*, yes, but a little taller than the ambassador had told him. Reading the look in his eyes she laughed.

"I stand upon my own feet, sir! I have no art to help me —I am neither taller nor shorter than this!"

She came only to his shoulder, and he was not a big man. But what they lacked in inches they made up in true royalty.

They went in to a good dinner of pheasant and venison. Her confessor—she had brought with her a numerous train of Capuchin monks as well as her French servants—reminded her that it was a fast day. Henrietta proceeded to enjoy the pheasant and the venison with a healthy fifteen-year-old appetite sharpened by sea air. There were times when she was meek and obedient to her priests and other times when she flouted them. The very marriage itself had taken place without waiting for the Pope's dispensation and she had been told to wait sixteen days at Amiens by way of penance, but she had been impatient. How could it be wrong to hasten to the man who was now her lawful husband? Skilfully avoiding the Pope's representative, Henrietta had sailed straight for England—and here she was.

They entered London by boat. The Thames was a better highway for a State entrance than any of the narrow streets ashore. They both wore green and stood beneath the canopy of the royal barge, for it had just been raining heavily. Now the June sky was brightening, the jumbled crooked roofs of London shone wetly, the houses on the Bridge were black with tiny figures, the grey ramparts of the Tower flared and thundered with saluting cannon. The twinkling river behind them was thronged with boats of every type, and each one packed to the water-line with cheering, waving Londoners. Apart from the official procession of barges, there were a thousand boats jostling their way upstream behind the bridal pair.

What was Charles feeling? He was touched and charmed by this kitten standing at his side. She was like his own mother in some ways—in her liveliness and frivolity, her lack of intellectual interests, her enthusiasm for masques and entertainments. She would be a queen of similar pattern, perhaps better. She had more sense of dignity for all her childishness. He could not see her upsetting people and making a fool of herself, as his mother had once done, by getting herself up, and her ladies, as blackamoors for a court entertainment. She had the inherited instincts of a French princess to help her there. Yes, he could safely leave her to run the social life of the court, to preside over all the gaieties and follies which bored him but seemed unavoidable.

But he was not in love with her, and it was a long time before real love came.

She vexed him by preferring her own French ladies to the English ones provided to attend her—yet she had some excuse, since the English language was unknown to her. She angered him more by her lack of respect for his own religion—she behaved as though it were not a religion at all, and her French monks encouraged her. Once (when he was away, himself) she and her ladies flounced through the assembled courtiers in the middle of their Church of England service, and back again, chattering noisily, a few minutes later. There were continual troubles. Worst of all, she could not be crowned Queen: she would not agree to a Protestant Archbishop and England would not agree to a Catholic, so that when Charles's coronation took place his wife could do no more than look down on the procession from a window like any other woman in London.

If Charles was gloomy and worried, Henrietta was still more unhappy. She could not understand this cold, reserved man who had married her. Did he know the meaning of love? He would light up with some enthusiasm if it was a question of horses or oil-paintings—yet did he really love *them*, or did he merely use the horses and collect the paintings? He was said to have such taste . . . Oh, for a little less taste, sighed Henrietta, and a little more warm emotion! At Christmas, bored and rebellious, she enjoyed a brief hour of revolt—muffling herself up like an ordinary London girl and slipping away into the crowded streets to see the shops. After a time she was recognised and had to make a hurried escape. Charles would not have approved of such goings-on. Of course, it had been all right for Charles and his precious Steenie to go, incognito, to Madrid!

They lived this strained, awkward life together for nearly a year. Then, one afternoon, Charles came into her apartments and found some of her French gentlemen playing the fool with more familiarity than was proper in the Queen's presence. There was a sudden hush. Seeing the thundercloud in the King's face the girl hastily changed her own smile to a more disapproving expression. Charles said nothing. He took her hand and led her coldly from the room. When they reached his own apartments he turned the key behind them and faced her.

It had got to stop, he told her. These Frenchmen must go, bag and baggage. Men, women, priests, the whole pack of them! She could keep her old nurse and her favourite dresser. The chefs could stay—they could do no harm in the kitchens. The rest must leave the palace now, this very moment, and they could lodge elsewhere until their journey to France could be arranged.

Henrietta forgot she was a Queen of England and a princess of France. She stormed and wept and screamed. When Charles went out, turning the key on her, she broke the window with her fist. The expelled French attendants looked up and saw her as they were driven out of the palace by the Yeomen of the Guard.

When she recovered from her rage, and her old retinue had left the country, Henrietta discovered that they had gone off with most of her own clothes. Perhaps, after all, Charles had been right in some of the things he had said about them! Perhaps, after all, Charles was a better man than she had suspected?

From that time the royal marriage entered a happier, warmer stage.

In after years Charles's reign was to be remembered as the era of the Civil War. It is often forgotten that most of his reign was outwardly peaceful, and that he ruled for seventeen years before there was talk of Cavaliers and Roundheads. Yet much happened in those seventeen years. More English emigrants sailed westwards to colonise America. Maryland was founded and named in honour of the Queen. Harvard was established, later to grow into the great American university. And eastwards the merchants of the East India Company opened the trading-post which was to become Calcutta, and laid the foundations of Britain's power in Asia. Charles built up the navy again, which his father had allowed to decay through too much economy. The *Sovereign of the Seas*, launched in 1637, was a great advance in ship-design. Charles was criticised for levying the tax called Ship-Money—but mainly by people who lived at a safe distance inland. Coast-dwellers were glad of protection against the Algerian pirates who, at the height of their power, came raiding even into the English Channel.

Meanwhile, ashore, much happened during those seventeen years. While the Dutchman Van Dyck painted Charles, his family, and the aristocracy of England, his fellow-countryman Vermuyden was draining the Fens and creating a great new tract of fertile farmland. Inigo Jones, the architect, was still alive and at work, nor was he the only man who could build: at Oxford, an unknown craftsman named Smith created the exquisite fan-vaulting over the staircase to Christ Church hall—not only one of the finest specimens of the style in the world but, most curiously, two hundred years later than the age to which that style belonged. Many a time was Charles to pass and repass beneath that vaulting, when Christ Church became his war-time home and he kept state in the noble hall at the top of those stairs. But the humble Smith's fan-vaulting was unusual in imitating bygone fashions. The new buildings of Charles's reign had their own individuality. It is to be seen in other Oxford colleges, notably in the second quadrangle of St. John's built by Archbishop Laud, and at Cambridge, as in the palatial splendour of Clare, and in country houses such as Raynham Hall in Norfolk. The other arts flourished. Charles himself was the greatest art-collector among all the English kings. There was much singing and playing, in and out of church: England, so musical under the Tudors, continued musical until the disapproving Puritans disbanded the choirs, pulled the organs out of the churches, banned Christmas carols and May Day dances, and frowned on most other forms of merrymaking.

As for literature, John Milton was writing the masque of *Comus* and the lament for *Lycidas*. Herrick and Herbert, Lovelace and Suckling, were pouring out shorter poems which still figure in every anthology. John Donne's strange, passionate verses, written many years earlier, were first published in 1633, just after his death. His biography was being written by his friend, a self-educated Fleet Street ironmonger, Izaak Walton, later to win fame as the author of *The Compleat Angler*. Sir Thomas Browne wrote *Religio Medici*. Ben Jonson and some of the other Elizabethan and Jacobean playwrights were still working for the six theatres that were now open in London, but younger dramatists such as Massinger, Ford and Shirley, were moving up into their places. The stage was active, but the new plays were only second-rate, as in Victorian England. Henrietta Maria, like the previous queen, preferred masques—not unnaturally, for both women were foreigners, and could never have fully grasped the rich spate of words poured out by a Shakespeare or a Marlowe. So the theatre, lacking the encouragement of court, played to the gallery.

Science was beginning to move out of the realm of superstition. Men were beginning to experiment, to correspond and exchange theories. Soon—in the year that Naseby was fought—they were to band themselves together more formally into "the Invisible College", which would develop later into the Royal Society. Men with inquiring minds were ready to look back as well as forwards, and Charles himself patronised archæology as a study "very useful to the general good of the State and Commonwealth".

There were changes in everyday life. Newspapers began in the first year of his reign, though their freedom of speech was strictly limited. The sedan chair appeared, soon to be followed by the stage coach.

Altogether, those seventeen years were not empty for England.

Nor were they empty years for the King and Queen. Gradually their state marriage became an affectionate personal one. Though they had the grief of losing their first baby at birth, and later two others, as was the common misfortune in those days, they had other children who grew up into a happy family—the boys and girls who were one day to be Charles II, Mary of Orange (mother of William III), and James II. Elizabeth died as a girl, and Henry, Duke of Gloucester, also died young, of smallpox, in the year of the Restoration. Later still, in 1644, came Charles II's favourite sister, Henrietta, nicknamed "Minette". There was no banishing of these children to distant guardians and governesses. Charles was devoted to them, supervising their lessons and forgetting his grave dignity to take part in their games.

The Queen had no reason now to be jealous of Steenie. Buckingham was stabbed by a discontented officer at Portsmouth, and died instantly. The news was brought to Charles as he knelt in chapel. He waved the messengers aside and continued in prayer without any sign of emotion, but, the service ended, shut himself away in a day-long agony of grief. He never had so close a friend again. His advisers became Archbishop Laud and Lord Strafford, but neither took the place of the gay Steenie, with whom he had once ridden out along the road to Spain.

Though the Civil War did not break out until 1642, all

those previous seventeen years were the preparation for it. Parliament was determined to control the country, Charles was equally determined to keep his "divine rights" intact for the kings who would follow him. Step by step, from the Petition of Right to the Grand Remonstrance, Parliament pushed him back. Step by step Charles retreated, until he felt the wall behind him and knew he could retreat no more. He was no tyrant by nature. He was ready to give way, for the sake of peace, on a number of issues. But there came a day when he knew he must fight, and another day when he knew he must die, rather than surrender on the main question.

Parliament sent Laud to prison and Strafford to the block. They had been Charles's loyal ministers, but he would not provoke the coming revolution by trying to save them. Full of remorse, deeply ashamed, he left the two men to their fate.

He tried to force the Prayer Book on Scotland, which had kept a separate Parliament and which he governed through a Secretary of State, hardly crossing the Border himself except for his Scottish coronation. The Scots rebelled and swore the Covenant to resist his form of religion. They invaded England. Charles had the pain of marching against his fellow-countrymen, and then the humiliation of having to give way to their demands.

It was Henrietta Maria, unused to the English and the Scots alike, accustomed only to the high-handed methods of foreign kings, who was continually goading him to defy his subjects. And it was Parliament's bold proposal to impeach her—to put the King's own wife on trial for her actions—that proved the last straw.

What follows is a familiar story. Henrietta taunted Charles. "Go, poltroon, pull these rogues by the ears—or see my face no more!" His pride stung, Charles strode across to Westminster, with his eleven-year-old son excitedly trotting at his heels, his nephew Prince Rupert (Elizabeth's dashing son), and five hundred soldiers at his back. He burst into the

F

House of Commons and tried to arrest the five members responsible for this insult to the Queen. If he had succeeded, the results would have been serious for him. But he failed —"the birds had flown"—and he was left to look ridiculous, which was worse.

That was January, 1642. In February Henrietta left England, making Charles promise to yield no more to Parliament until she returned. She was taking their daughter Mary to Holland. The rest of the children stayed with their father. For the next six months Charles and his enemies gathered their forces for the battle which was now certain, but which neither wished to begin. On 22nd August, on a hillock outside Nottingham Castle, Charles raised his standard with the device, *Give Cæsar his due.* The Civil War had begun.

Edgehill, Marston Moor, Naseby . . . Prince Rupert, Fairfax, Oliver Cromwell and his Ironsides . . . No need to re-tell here the story of the war. It is in every school history-book of England.

When not riding with his troops, Charles spent most of those years at the royalist headquarters in Oxford. Wolsey's magnificent college, Christ Church, became his palace. The Cavalier minority held their own "parliament" in its hall, and the chapel, already doing double duty as Oxford Cathedral, became also the King's place of worship. Council meetings were held at Oriel College near-by, and Henrietta, when she ran the gauntlet of the Roundheads and got back from abroad, had her apartments over the archway at Merton, with a private way made for her into Christ Church through Corpus Christi, the small college sandwiched between. As a rest from cares of state, Charles found delight in the quiet gardens of the university or amid the bookshelves of the Bodleian Library.

But the war, after beginning well, went badly. First there was the defeat at Marston Moor. Oxford became less safe, and Henrietta was sent down into the West Country. Charles rode out with her the first few miles, and their farewells were made in the little Berkshire town of Abingdon. Later Henrietta went to France—she was ill and her nerve was breaking—and so she never saw his face again.

Cromwell's triumph at Naseby broke the main Cavalier army. But Charles remembered that he was still King of England, not a defeated foreign general. His enemies were not united. The Parliament was jealous of its own army leaders, and the Scots army, brought into England as their allies, had a hand of its own to play. Charles was like a man whose sword is broken but whose wits are still sharp. Might he not continue the struggle by political bargaining?

The Scots seemed his best hope. A month before Oxford surrendered to the Roundheads, a disguised king slipped out of the city before dawn and hurried northwards to the Scots army in Nottinghamshire. There followed nine months of weary conferences. At the finish the Scots cautiously decided they would strike a better bargain with Parliament. They sold Charles for £200,000, that being the amount of their back pay handed over to them by the Roundheads.

That was January, 1647. For the next two years Charles was kept prisoner in various places and under different conditions. Sometimes he was closely watched and strictly confined; at others he was treated with great respect and allowed freedom for exercise and amusement. At one stage he was able to hunt and play tennis, and have his younger children, James, Elizabeth, and Henry, lodging near-by. Once, in Hampshire, he escaped and was at large for some time, trying to get a boat to the Channel Isles, but he was recaptured before he could do so. A second attempt, to get out of Carisbrooke Castle in the Isle of Wight, failed at the last moment because Charles, small though he was, could not squeeze his shoulders through the narrow window of his room. When a third chance of freedom came it was too late: by then Charles had given his parole, and, though an easy means of escape was open, he refused to break his royal word of honour.

In 1648 the war flared up again. There were Cavalier risings in Wales and Essex, and the Scots, switching sides, came over the Border again—only to be smashed by Cromwell at the battle of Preston Moor. In a sense it was his supporters who sealed Charles's fate. The extreme parliamentary party felt there would be no certain peace while Charles lived. It was decided to try him and put him to death.

Charles was not the only man who believed that a king could not be tried in this way, and that no earthly court could sit in judgment upon him. The famous parliamentary general, Fairfax, was only one of many sincere Roundheads who would have nothing to do with the proceedings. The trial was forced through by a ruthless and determined group, claiming to represent the people of England but actually forming only a minority of a minority of a Parliament elected (by a minority of the population) nine years before.

In January, 1649, Charles faced his accusers in the Great Hall of Westminster. He sat on a velvet-covered chair, a smallish, dark-clad figure, fingering a cane with a silver knob. Silvering too was his hair, though he was still on the young side of fifty, but few were near enough to see, for he kept his hat on, as was common indoor practice in that century. The years of care had sharpened the lines of his face.

Though he refused to plead either "guilty" or "not guilty" —since he could not agree that the trial was legal—he did not remain silent. For a whole week he stubbornly argued the point at every opportunity. No one, even his scholarly father, was better equipped by now to discuss a king's position in relation to the law and the people. And James could never have backed his learning with the courage and dignity which his son now showed on the threshold of death.

It was all of no avail. The result of the trial had been decided by his enemies even before it began. On the last day the sentence was pronounced, "that the said Charles Stuart, as a tyrant, traitor, murderer and a public enemy, shall be put to death by the severing his head from his body". Charles made a last appeal for the right to speak, was refused, and hustled away by the pikemen guarding him. "I am not suffered for to speak," he said quietly. "Expect what justice *other* people will have!" There was a sedan chair waiting outside. The chair-men doffed their hats respectfully, but the soldiers roughly quelled this, and all other signs of sympathy for the prisoner.

That was Saturday. The execution was fixed for the following Tuesday morning, on a scaffold to be erected in front of the palace of Whitehall. Charles spent the week-end settling the small affairs of this world and preparing himself for the next. He had been allowed to have his dogs with him to the end, Gipsy the greyhound and his spaniel Rogue. They would be sent to Henrietta in France. Young Charles should have his Bible, and James a little silver sundial—James too was safe overseas by now, he had been spirited away by loyal friends during a carefully-timed game of hide-and-seek. Elizabeth and Henry were still in London. They were brought to say good-bye. There were books and trinkets for them. There were other gifts of watches, rings, and such like to his most faithful friends.

His one remaining worry was that he should not behave with proper dignity in the last awful scene on that stage lifted above the crowd at Whitehall. He was going to his death deliberately, for the things in which he sincerely believed. There had been many occasions when he could have avoided this fate, if he had been willing to give up his beliefs. But he had kept faith with his father's teaching, kept faith with his successors as yet unborn.

As a child, stammering and unsure of his steps, he had striven so hard to be worthy of his princely rank. As a boy, the younger weakly brother of the heroic Henry, he had dreamed wistfully of action and glory on distant battlefields. Now he needed a colder courage.

"Death is not terrible to me," he assured Bishop Juxon. "I bless my God, I am prepared." He was only afraid of *seeming* afraid. He put on extra clothes lest the bitter January morning should make him shiver, and the crowd not understand.

"Remember," he said quietly to the Bishop, handing him as a keepsake the silver-knobbed cane. The black-draped platform waited outside the tall window through which he must presently go. The crowd waited, among them a fifteen-year-old St. Paul's schoolboy, Samuel Pepys, who would one day recall the morning in his diary and how, less than a dozen years later, he saw the beginning of other executions at Charing Cross, "the first blood shed in revenge for the King". The troopers waited, their faces grim under the steel peaks of their helmets, ready to crush any disorder in favour of Charles.

"I go from a corruptible crown to an incorruptible one," said Charles quietly to the Bishop, when the latter fumbled for words of comfort. The moment had come. Charles stepped out into the wintry air. His dignity never faltered for an instant. It was all finished very quickly. There was no cheer from the crowd, only a low gasp of horror as the executioner displayed the royal head. The Ironsides, thankful for an excuse to do something, spurred their horses forward and began, roughly, to break up the unresisting, quietly muttering crowd.

Charles the King was no more. But in that moment, in the hearts of many, Charles the Martyr was born.

6

Charles II: King of Hearts—or Knave?

A BOY snatched pen and paper, signed his name at the bottom of a blank sheet, and sent it by urgent courier to England. Let Parliament fill in whatever conditions it liked, he would honour that signature. If only they would spare his father's life!

The hot-blooded human gesture (so different from what his father would have done) had no effect. While the exiles at the French court were still numbed by the pronouncement of the death-sentence, there followed the almost unbelievable news that the sentence had been carried out.

King Charles was dead. A sallow, ugly boy of eighteen found his friends and companions kneeling to kiss his hand, and hailing him by his new title.

King Charles II . . . Fated to go down in history as "the merry monarch". But at that moment the grief-shattered boy could think of only one thing: revenge.

Something of his life, up to that moment, has been indicated in the previous chapter. The loving, so different, parents— grave, rather cold father, and gay, frivolous, hot-tempered mother; the happy family-circle of younger brothers and sisters; the elegance of court, with its masques and music, its talk of art and architecture; the horses and hounds, the spaniels and other dogs; and then the sad changes and anxieties of the war years.

This second Charles had been born on 29th May, 1630—

"so ugly", laughed his young mother ruefully, "that I am ashamed of him". It was no doubt from her side of the family that he got his swarthy skin, just as he got his lazy good humour and full-blooded passions rather from the south of France than from the north of Britain.

His first memories were of an outwardly happy England, in which only the most far-seeing of men could observe the creeping shadow of the Civil War. When he turned from baby's rattle to small boy's drum and hobby-horse, few realised how soon the country would be echoing to the thunder of real drums and charging cavalry. When he was six, his big cousin Rupert, then seventeen, came over for a visit and fell in love with the country as he saw it then. Going for a last ride on the day he left, Rupert cried out that he would not mind breaking his neck, if it meant staying in England for ever. Such was the sunny world of Charles's childhood.

Quaintly enough, out of all the playthings and pets at his disposal, the little prince lavished his strongest affections on a simple block of wood, and insisted on taking it to bed with him as though he could not bear to sleep alone.

Like most royal children, he knew a variety of homes. Sometimes the family were at Whitehall, sometimes they went down-river to stay at Greenwich or up-river to Hampton Court; at other times they were at Windsor. When he was eight, he was solemnly created a Knight of the Garter and given his own household, with the Earl of Newcastle and the Bishop of Chichester to supervise his education. This did not mean that his parents neglected him; they kept a close watch on his upbringing, and there is a sorrowful letter from the Queen still in existence, threatening to come over herself and make him take his medicine if he will not swallow it at the Earl's bidding.

Charles liked medicine as little as do most children. A short while afterwards, when the Earl was away, he wrote him a respectful letter with all the craftiness of an eight-year-old:

> *"My Lord,*
> *"I would not have you take too much physic, for it does always make me worse and I think it will do the like with you. I ride every day and am ready to follow any other directions from you. Make haste to return to him that loves you.*
>
> *"Charles P."*

His mother might have smiled to read that letter. It was her great concern that Charles should develop the tact and ease of manner which her husband lacked. He was to study people rather than books. The Earl of Newcastle was completely in sympathy with this idea of education. The boy's weakness at Latin did not matter. The only subject really worth hard study was history, because history taught one about men and how to handle them.

Charles's little note about the medicine shows how promising a pupil he was from the first. If the power to charm men and women were the only object of education, his early training would have been a triumphant success.

What his father most admired in Newcastle was his horsemanship. The Earl was one of the outstanding horsemen in Europe. Riding was, as the prince's letter shows, part of the daily routine. It led to a broken arm when he was eleven and came off somewhat heavily in Hyde Park. He was never his father's equal in the saddle, but like all the Stuarts (even his learned grandfather, James) he was keenly interested in horses. But it was racing even more than stag-hunting which appealed to him, and it was he, when he grew up, who developed Newmarket into the famous sporting centre it has been ever since. One of his nicknames, "Old Rowley", was taken from a fine stallion belonging to the royal stud.

Riding was not his only exercise. Like his father he

enjoyed tennis, the strenuous indoor tennis of those days. He fenced and danced. He was not bookish but he had wide interests, as he showed later, notably by his amateur dabblings in science. He loved music, but his tastes were light; he preferred a tune he could beat time to.

From an early age he showed a keen sense of humour—if at times a rather coarse one. That humour never deserted him, even on his death-bed.

He was to need it in the difficult years which now lay before him.

Charles was twelve when the Civil War began.

Too young to fight yet, he stayed close at his father's heels, as he had done on that day when they had marched across to the House of Commons and tried to arrest the five members. The King wanted him under his eye. He was haunted by a fear that the Roundheads would get hold of the boy and use him either as a hostage or as a puppet-king in opposition to himself.

Young Charles watched the first battle, Edgehill, from the steep Warwickshire hillside above. His little brother James was with him, and they were in the charge of the King's doctor, the famous William Harvey, who discovered the circulation of the blood. Dr. Harvey sat on the grass calmly reading a book, indifferent to the blood which was flowing so tragically on the battlefield below. Only when some shots pattered dangerously near did he jump to his feet and lead his protesting companions further up the hill.

Charles revelled in the rough fun of campaigning. He liked mixing with the common soldiers—he was never a snob—and it was noticed, with some dismay, how readily he picked up the bad language and broad jokes which were bandied round the camp-fires.

He spent the next year or two with his parents in Oxford. When the war took a turn for the worse and his mother went abroad, Charles was sent to Bristol for greater safety. The King had changed his mind now. It was better for the Prince of Wales to be in another place. He himself might be captured. The boy must not be captured too.

With the fifteen-year-old prince he sent a remarkable man, Edward Hyde. Hyde was a lawyer and a Member of Parliament. He did not believe in the divine right of kings but in a proper partnership between King and Parliament. He had voted, in his time, with the King's most bitter opponents, but when matters had come to actual warfare he had joined the royalists. The King had seen his great abilities, despite their differences of opinion. In trusting the prince to Hyde, he ensured (without realising it) that his son would one day be welcomed back to London and would die peacefully in his bed, instead of on a scaffold like himself. For two things were to make the second Charles acceptable to the people: his personality and the influence Hyde had exerted upon his political behaviour. Not that the second Charles was ever to show any enthusiasm for Hyde's notions of working in partnership with Parliament—he liked his own way as much as ever his father had done, but at least he learnt from Hyde that he could not expect to get it.

Later, Hyde was to become the Earl of Clarendon and to write the classic *History of the Rebellion*. He was also, though he did not live to see it, to become the grandfather of two English monarchs, for—flat against his wishes—his daughter married Charles's young brother James, the Duke of York, in 1660. It was their children who were later crowned as Queen Mary II and Queen Anne respectively.

All this was hidden in the future—and very well hidden—when Charles said good-bye to his father and started for Bristol. With the war going so badly, no one could be sure that England would ever see another coronation at all.

Defeat followed defeat. Hyde took Charles to the Scilly Isles for safety, thence to Jersey, and at last, when the war seemed lost, to the French court at the Louvre, where his mother was living. The period of exile had begun.

There was a dramatic break in that period, when he was twenty-one.

Scotland was always the doubtful factor in the situation, for she was still an independent kingdom, and her support shifted from one side to the other in the English struggle. Having handed over Charles I to the English Parliament only a few years before, the Scots now swung round to Charles II. A bargain was struck with the young exile. He landed in Scotland, and was duly crowned king of that country at Scone, the traditional spot for such a ceremony. Then, with a Scottish army at his back, Charles rode southwards into England.

He had hoped that the English Cavaliers would flock to his standard, but the people were war-weary and many were disgusted by the behaviour of the Scots, whom they looked upon as foreign invaders. Charles had planned a clear run through to London, for he had left Cromwell behind in Scotland with the main Roundhead army. But, with only a trickle of recruits coming in and a number of the Scots already deserting with their plunder, he realised that he would be heading for disaster. He paused, therefore, in the royalist city of Worcester, believing that with time he could build up his forces. Unfortunately that time was even more useful to the Roundheads. Cromwell was in hot pursuit. Other troops were mustering. A net of swords was closing in upon the young King.

He set up his standard in Worcester on the 22nd August, the ninth anniversary of that fateful day when his father's had been unfurled at Nottingham. But Cromwell too had a taste for anniversaries. He chose to launch his attack on 3rd September, exactly one year after his victory over the Scots at Dunbar.

Charles knew that he was outnumbered two to one. To make up for this, he used the River Severn to divide his enemies. He, having command of the city bridge, could move his men quickly from one bank to the other as necessary. Cromwell, now moving up-stream from the south, must have troops on either side; but, not having control of a bridge, he would not be able to shift reinforcements quickly from the one bank to the other. Being Cromwell, however, the military genius of his age, he found his own way out of the difficulty.

Charles spent the morning of the battle riding round the lines. All was quiet. He was just finishing a meal at his headquarters when distant firing was heard. He hurried out and climbed to the top of the cathedral tower. It was then, probably, that he got his first inkling of Cromwell's daring plan. The Roundhead leader had collected twenty broad river-boats and had them towed up-stream against the powerful current. By laying planks across them a pontoon-bridge had been built, under the very noses of the defenders. Cromwell could now move his men to and fro as easily as Charles could—and he had twice as many to play with.

Charles did not despair. In this, his first and last battle as a commander, he showed skill as well as courage. He did not do the obvious thing. He could see that Cromwell was piling up strength on the western bank, but he did not send his own reserves scurrying over to meet them. Better, first, to strike at his enemy's weak point on the eastern bank.

Clattering down from the cathedral-tower, he sprang into the saddle, gathered every available man, and led them in a furious sortie through the city-gate. His bold stroke almost succeeded. The Roundheads, taken by surprise, reeled back in disorder. Only Cromwell could have saved the situation, which he did by galloping across the pontoon-bridge and appearing to rally his stricken right wing. All that September afternoon the battle raged, until dusk came down upon the defeat of the royalists. The Scottish cavalry, having already refused to charge with the King, now fled along the darkening road to the north, leaving the infantry to save themselves if they could. And Charles, having fought gallantly throughout, found himself the most keenly hunted of all the fugitives.

The story of the next six weeks is one of the classics of "escape" literature, and it would take the whole length of this book to do justice to it.

With a reward of a thousand pounds upon his head (a vast price for those days), Charles wandered north into Shropshire and Staffordshire, then south again to Bristol, and finally eastwards into Sussex.

His dark hair was clumsily cut with the aid of shears and pudding-basin, and his Cavalier finery was exchanged for the drab, threadbare suit of a country servant. Once his borrowed shoes were so painful that he threw them away and walked in his stockings until his bleeding feet could carry him no further. He had to skulk along hedgerows and lie hidden in the woods. One Catholic family concealed him—though himself no Catholic—in their secret priest-hole. In another house he curled up to sleep in the narrow space beneath the attic-floor. Most famous of all his refuges was the hollow oak at Boscobel, where, worn out by his hardships, he dozed in the arms of a comrade while the Roundhead soldiers scoured the wood around him.

Even ordinary people needed passes to travel along the roads. One of the royalists, Colonel Lane, had a sister who had obtained a permit to visit a sick friend near Bristol. It was arranged that Charles should travel with her party, disguised as her man-servant, "William Jackson". Jane Lane, a pretty, dark girl, was in the secret, but even her mother did not know who "Jackson" really was. Jane rode pillion behind him, and in this fashion they travelled down the Cotswolds and into Somerset.

Arrived there, after some narrow escapes, Charles found it still impossible to get abroad. He said a reluctant farewell to Jane and turned eastwards through Dorset and the other counties of the south coast. One set of friends passed him on to another. There was even a second spell of pillion-riding, this time with the attractive Juliana Coningsby to share his horse. There were breathless moments of danger, unbearable hours of anxious waiting. And there were odd spells of relaxation (as when he went to see the wonders of Stonehenge), and incidents to tickle his ironical sense of humour. Thus, on one occasion, a drunken Cavalier spent some time vainly trying to convert the sober-looking young stranger to his own royalist opinions; and on another, when a false report had reached the district that Charles Stuart was captured and killed, Charles was able to look out of the window and watch the villagers dancing round a bonfire to celebrate the news.

Finally, in the middle of October, a little ship was found, and he was able to flit across the Channel to France. The brig which carried him was named, not unsuitably, the *Surprise*.

For the next eight years Charles and his group of faithful followers knew the real bitterness of exile. They had hopes, still, but those hopes were dimmer and more distant than they had been before the adventure at Worcester.

Was there any positive certainty that they would ever get back? Foreign governments, though horrified by the death of the late king and sympathetic to his son, were afraid of Cromwell and did not much fancy Charles's chances against him. Under the Lord Protector, this Commonwealth of England was more of a force to be reckoned with than at any time since the days of Queen Elizabeth. As always in history, the nations considered their own interests first. For the time being, at least, they preferred to take no risks by showing too much friendliness to the young exile.

Charles and his friends were almost penniless. The wealth of the royal family and its supporters had long since gone to pay for the war—it had gone up in the smoke of Marston Moor and Naseby. Gold and silver plate had been melted down, jewellery had been sold to the merchants of Antwerp and Amsterdam. Charles lived in shabby lodgings, ate in cheap taverns, and went short of firewood in the winter-time. Fortunately his good-humour never deserted him. He had a taste for low life, he enjoyed rubbing shoulders with the common people, and he could bear a mode of existence at which his refined father would have shuddered.

He was alive. And life was good, even under these conditions. He was young, and a pretty girl was always a pretty girl, even though one's pockets were too light to lavish presents on her.

Hyde cocked a disapproving eye upon Charles's flirtations and amusements. He would have preferred the King to behave more respectably and think of his reputation, so that it would be easier some day to regain the support of the sober English people. Some of the exiles were jealous of Hyde's influence. One, trying to make mischief, burst out at the Council table. Charles should know what Hyde was saying about his behaviour.

Charles laughed. "That's no news," he said, his good temper quite unruffled. "He has told me so twenty times to my face."

From eighteen onwards, he was in and out of love innumerable times. His first serious affair was with Lucy Walter, daughter of a Cavalier fugitive, and described as "a brown, beautiful, bold but insipid creature". Many years later it was her son, the Duke of Monmouth, who led the rebellion against James II which ended in the Battle of Sedgmoor.

Lucy Walter was the first. Others followed, at all too-frequent intervals, throughout his life. Nell Gwynne, the theatre orange-girl, is the best remembered—and best deserves to be, if her warm heart and human kindliness, her wit and her beauty, may be set against her not-so-strict behaviour. All too well Charles had learnt the lesson of getting on with people, as his mother had wished him to, but it was always with the other sex that he preferred to exercise his skill.

There was one pleasant and quite innocent little interlude during this period. Jane Lane made her reappearance, for England had become uncomfortable for so royalist a girl. Charles heard she was coming to Paris and rode out to meet her, embraced her warmly, and told everyone how she had saved his life. In his poverty there was little he could do to help her, but he got his sister Mary, who was married to the Prince of Orange, to make her a lady-in-waiting. Jane went to her new post in Holland and for years afterwards she and Charles wrote to each other as friends. He never forgot those days when they had ridden pillion as mistress and servant, and when he required an alias, as he moved about Europe secretly, it amused him to become "Mr. Jackson" again.

These secret movements were part of what we should call, today, the "counter-revolution". The most determined royalists were banded together in an underground organisation known as the Sealed Knot. They were continually planning armed risings in England. A stream of their agents was for ever trickling through the watchful defences of the Commonwealth. Overseas, the struggle against Cromwell was carried on by every possible means from the stirring up of resistance in the colonies to the assassination of his ambassadors at foreign courts.

Charles and his supporters could not be expected to see English history as it would be seen by later generations. To them Cromwell was, quite plainly, a traitor, a murderer, and a tyrant. Each new wave of escaping royalists brought fresh news and rumours of the state into which England was fallen. They told of army mutinies and arrests, of closed theatres and disbanded choirs, of deserted race-courses and forbidden amusements. They said less about the other side of the picture—how the roads were now much clearer of highway-men, how there was more toleration now for the persecuted Quakers, how there were schemes afoot for simplifying the law so that the common man could understand it, for treating lunatics more humanely, and for making other reforms.

One thing, above all, provoked the savage amusement of the exiled Cavaliers. Had not the Civil War been fought to prove that Parliament was even more sacred than the King? Yet what had Cromwell done at the finish? He had disbanded his precious Parliament, turned them out of doors as his late Majesty would never have dreamt of doing, and set up a military dictatorship in their place! Was not England now parcelled out into districts, each ruled by a major-general with more absolute power than any king?

Charles and his threadbare court moved like gipsies through a nervous and unfriendly Europe. Now at Cologne, now at Bruges, now at Brussels. He was playing tennis in the country not far from this last city when an excited courtier burst in upon the game. The unbelievable had happened. Cromwell, only fifty-eight, with many possible years of vigour before him, had died—supreme irony, on 3rd September, the anniversary of his victories at Dunbar and Worcester, the day he had himself called "the crowning mercy".

Was this to be a crowning mercy in another sense? Was his death going to crown Charles? After the first delirious rejoicings were over, the exiles had more than a year of weary waiting. Richard Cromwell took his father's place—but only in name, for "Queen Dick" had none of Oliver's personality. Affairs in England drifted into more and more confusion. The thieves were falling out, laughed the exiled Cavaliers; soon the honest men would come into their own. As the disunity grew in England, so did the hopes of the English-men watching from abroad.

It was a general who settled the question. General Monk, sensing the mood of the nation, marched down from the

Scottish Border, took control of London, and ordered a general election. It was obvious that the new Parliament would vote to recall Charles to the throne. Without violence the power slipped from one side to the other. For all the endless debates and documents of those complicated days, the essence of the matter was contained in the song the London apprentices were singing in the streets:

> *"Ding a ding ding, I heard a bird sing,*
> *The Parliament soldiers are gone to the king!"*

And the sailors had gone *for* the King.

Charles had left England in a little brig sailed by two men and a boy: he was brought back from Holland by the whole fleet, sailing across the North Sea, a splendid forest of canvas rippling in the May sunshine. James and Henry were to go with him. Mary and his Aunt Elizabeth came aboard to kiss him good-bye. The flagship, formerly the *Naseby*, was quickly and tactfully renamed the *Royal Charles*. Among the crowd of gentlemen on the deck was a young clerk to the Admiralty, that very Samuel Pepys who, as a schoolboy, had watched the execution of the late king. Charles was scarcely aware of his smiling, over-anxious face—there were so many faces that day, all smiling and most of them anxious —but in due time he was to know Mr. Pepys quite well. What he was never to know, and what no man then living was to know, was that Mr. Pepys would record his impression of that day in a secret diary, which no other eye would read until the nineteenth century.

Charles was now within a week of his thirtieth birthday. The sallow, ugly boy had grown into a heavy-featured man who, if not handsome, had a kind of devil-like distinction which appealed more to some people than ordinary good looks. "The Black Boy", some called him. He had the air of a rascal—but at least he was a rascal with an air.

A sardonic smile curved his lips as England battered him with cheers and gun-salutes and deafening peals of bells. He had been a fool, he remarked to one companion, not to have come back sooner. Did not every man he met assure him that he, personally, had been only waiting for this day?

Charles accepted the welcome but he was not fooled by it. Things were not going to be easy. He had one foot in the stirrup of his kingdom: he had yet to show that he could ride the unruly, plunging horse that was the English people.

On one point he was determined: he was not going to lose his head as his father had done, nor was he prepared to "go on his travels again". He was going to be charming to everybody. In some cases the charm came more naturally than others. He quite enjoyed eating the ordinary sailors' breakfast of pork and peas and boiled beef: it took a little more effort to embrace General Monk on Dover beach and call him "father", to pay flattering attentions to Mrs. Monk, and to assure the Mayor that he loved the Bible "above all things in the world". But he played his part—tirelessly, one would have said, if there was not evidence how exhausted he was by the end of that first day. It lies in the note he sent to his favourite sister, Minette, before he tumbled wearily into bed at Canterbury:

"My head is so dreadfully stunned with the acclamations of the people, and the vast amount of business, that I know not whether I am writing sense or nonsense."

Every man in the country seemed to be crowding forward to impress his face and name upon the new King. Those who had been abroad for any reason all insisted that they had been sharers in his exile and, having sacrificed everything in the cause, deserved reward. And those who had stayed behind in England were most anxious to point out that they had done so for the best possible motives. Poor Mr. Pepys was sadly embarrassed about this time when he met an old schoolfellow who *"did remember that I was a great Roundhead when I was a boy*", and there were plenty of public men with much more recent and serious miscalculations which they were anxious to forget.

It was, of course, utterly impossible for Charles to undo the ruin of the past eighteen years. He did what he could to reward his loyal supporters and he was particularly generous to those whose claims he knew personally to be genuine. Once more Jane Lane flits across the stage of history: he gave her a pension and a number of expensive presents. But the whole kingdom could not be turned upside-down to put everyone back where he had been in 1642.

When it came to punishing the Roundhead leaders, Charles found that the fire of his revenge had burnt low. It was not he, but the new Parliament, that insisted on the barbaric digging up and exhibiting of Cromwell's body at Tyburn, and the still more barbaric execution of General Harrison and the other surviving ringleaders in the killing of his father. Even so, when less than half the executions had been carried out, he saved the rest of the prisoners by a note to Hyde: "*I confess I am weary of hanging—let it sleep.*" With great difficulty he persuaded his supporters to allow a free pardon to everyone else who had served on the other side.

There had been enough bloodshed.

One of his first moves—it was also partly for economy— was to disband the fine army which Cromwell had created. But some troops he had to have, if only to defend his person against assassins and rioters, so very soon he formed the Life Guards, with the breast-plates, scarlet coats, white plumes, and jack boots which have developed into the uniform we see today. A few years later came the Grenadiers. His name is thus associated with the oldest regiments in the British Army; and also (which is in keeping with the warm kindliness of his character) the Chelsea Hospital for "old soldiers broken in the wars".

.   .   .   .   .

Then, as now, the Life Guards stood sentinel at Whitehall. But the Whitehall of Charles II was still the great rambling royal palace where his father had kept court.

The young man who, not so long ago, had eaten cheap meals in the taverns of Paris now dined in solitary state in the vast banqueting hall which Inigo Jones had designed under the inspiration of the classical ruins he had seen in Italy. Solitary, because he had as yet no queen to sit beside him, and, save when he had royal guests to share his meal, he must eat alone: all the splendid and noble figures crowding the scene were there only to stand and wait, or to offer him dishes, humbly kneeling. That was court etiquette, and it made little appeal to Charles. He liked to slip away as soon as the last mouthful was swallowed. He looked forward to the evenings, when he could lay aside this ceremony and relax at private supper-parties.

It was easy to be lonely in Whitehall, but difficult to be alone.

If he came in from riding, the long Stone Gallery leading to his apartments was thronged with people hoping to catch his ear for a moment and beg some favour. The place was as public as an art gallery—which was just, in fact, what his picture-collecting father had made of it. For all his warmth and generosity, for all his sympathy with ordinary people, Charles was often compelled to stride through the bowing crowd as fast as he could, ignoring the pathetic eye, the eager smile, and the outstretched paper.

When he had run the gauntlet and slipped past the sentries by the velvet-hung doors into the withdrawing-room, he could enjoy only what generals call a very "limited withdrawal". Innumerable courtiers had the right to enter there. Many, indeed, had the right to follow him into his bed-chamber beyond, a large room overlooking the Thames, where he dealt with state business not handled at his Council table; but here he could, at least, exclude others while he held confidential talks with one or two.

CHARLES II

For real privacy he must mount a few stairs and unlock the door of the King's closet. It was the kind of room which today gets termed a "den". It was full of clocks and watches, which he loved collecting. They were all ticking away but they did not always agree, so, distrusting so great a variety of opinions, he used to set his own watch every morning, if the sun shone, by the sundial in the Privy Gardens. Here in the Closet were his other collections—model ships, maps, pictures, jewels, *objets d'art*. Personal friends would be taken in to see these, but only one other man had a key to that locked door—the discreet and faithful Will Chiffinch, officially a "page" of the bedchamber but in years old enough to be his father. Chiffinch knew most, if not all, of his secrets, but no man knew better how to hold his tongue.

One hobby Charles could not practise safely among all these art treasures—and that was chemistry. He had his laboratory immediately below his Closet, so it was perhaps as well that he did not experiment with anything too explosive. He liked to dispense medicines and cordials of his own devising, growing herbs for the purpose in a part of the palace-grounds known as the Physic Garden. It was not an unusual interest for a man of his rank and period. Even his adventurous cousin Rupert turned to it in his later years.

Science was in the air. The "Invisible College" founded in his father's time was about to blossom forth, under Charles's encouragement, into the Royal Society we know today. Newton the mathematician, Halley the astronomer, Boyle the chemist, and Wren the many-sided genius who finally concentrated on architecture—these were only four outstanding figures among a crowd of alert and able men who made this the first great period of scientific progress in England.

Charles himself, of course, had neither the time nor the intellect to follow them into the higher realms of speculation. Apart from State business, too many other interests called him. Few men lived more fully.

Puritans—and even less strait-laced people—might shake their heads over his late nights and candle-lit supper-parties. None the less, the King was often up and playing tennis by six o'clock in the morning, or galloping along the road to Hampton Court at five. With James he would go swimming in the Thames at Putney or Battersea (Henry, alas, died of smallpox a few months after the three royal brothers regained their childhood home); and he was never happier than when he was afloat, sailing a new type of craft called a "yacht" presented to him by the Dutch government, or the improved version of it which was quickly designed by the famous English shipbuilder, Peter Pett. Other days found him riding after the stag or running with old Chiffinch's beagles. He was nearly forty-five when, after three keenly-contested heats, he rode the winner himself in the Newmarket Plate. No man as fit as Charles could be accused of ruining his health by late hours and riotous living.

He loved the fresh air, whether it carried the scent of grass and flowers or the salty tang of the sea. London smoke, already a nuisance, he hated. Sportsman though he was, he liked the gentler exercise as well, strolling in park and garden with people to talk to and his dogs rollicking at his heels. It is to Charles that Londoners owe the artificial lake in St. James's Park and the oldest of the trees that grow there. He was the first to stock the park with birds and went to feed the ducks like any modern visitor. But he maintained a miniature zoo there, as well, with antelopes and deer and other animals.

Indoors, he liked good talk, dancing, gay music, and the theatre. The stately masques continued, as in his mother's and his grandmother's day, but Charles preferred the public playhouses in Drury Lane and Lincoln's Inn Fields. Here, after the long Puritan ban, the English drama was born anew and utterly different. Gone were the last lovely fancies of the Shakespearean age. Prose took the place of poetry, just as bold-eyed actresses took over the female parts once played by boys. Cynical, coarse wit and worldly wisdom took the place of romance. It was the mood of the court. Only a few older people sighed for the old-fashioned plays of their youth. Was one, perhaps, his own aunt Elizabeth, who remembered the first production of a comedy called *The Tempest*, and being told that the girl-heroine, Miranda, was intended for herself? Yet the Restoration drama, though little more than tarnished silver beside the pure gold of the best earlier plays, made its own contribution to the total wealth of English literature.

Such, then, was the day-to-day life of the King.

It did not alter much after he married.

A king in those days could not expect to marry for love. He must wed some foreign princess, whom perhaps he had never seen, so that their two countries could benefit from the alliance. The best he could hope for was to fall in love with her later. That happened quite often. It had happened to the first Charles.

After just two years of bachelor kingship, Charles chose a Portuguese princess, Catherine of Braganza, as his bride. She was a dark, dainty, rather solemn little thing. Her teeth were a shade prominent, but she had beautiful hands, and in her rose-coloured wedding-dress, with her dark eyes liquid and bright with the excitement of it all, she was not unattractive. She brought with her as dowry the port of Tangier in Morocco, opposite Gibraltar, and the Portuguese settlement at Bombay, which was to prove most valuable to British trade with India.

Charles rode to meet her at Portsmouth, where she had just landed, still queasy after the voyage from Lisbon. The next morning they were married secretly, to please her, by a Roman Catholic priest, and after dinner publicly, to please the nation, by a bishop of the Church of England. A few days later they set out for Hampton Court for their honeymoon. May was just turning into June, the weather was kind, and the place was looking its best. They were able to have picnics and to go boating. Coming from Portugal, Catherine was delighted by the freshness of the early summer flowers and the sheer greenness of English lawns and leaves.

She fell in love with Charles. For him, the miracle never happened. He could never surrender his heart to her as he could to others. He treated her with a strange mixture of kindness and cruelty—at times going to great lengths of tenderness and consideration, at others almost breaking her heart by his thoughtless and unfeeling behaviour. Catherine took him as she found him, wayward, faithless, yet somehow always at the end forgivable. She put up with everything and gave him a life-long affection in return.

Matters might have gone differently if they had had children. As it was, most of the reign was clouded by the background problem of the succession. If Charles died without an heir, the crown would pass to his brother. James was a staunch Roman Catholic and would never, like Charles, play the hypocrite in religion to please the people. All that Parliament could do was to insist that James's little daughters, Mary and Anne, should be brought up in the Church of England. Charles often warned his brother that, unless he learnt to handle the English more skilfully, he would lose his head or at least his crown, and it took the obstinate James only four years as king to prove him right.

Charles himself was a pastmaster in handling his turbulent subjects. He had his own strong views, but he always knew when to give way gracefully if it was unavoidable.

For the first seven years, while he was settling himself in the saddle, he let Hyde run things pretty much his own way. But he had no real use for Hyde's theory of a partnership between King and Parliament; when Hyde grew old, pompous, and dogmatic, and had made himself unpopular with everyone, Charles took the reins in his own hands.

In his heart he wanted to be a despot (though a benevolent one) like his cousin, King Louis XIV, across the Channel. Charles loved everything French. France was, after all, his mother's country and now the home of Minette, who was married to the French king's brother. It was the country where, despite shortage of cash, he had spent some merry times as a young exile. It was the land of good breeding and polished manners, of civilisation and elegance. Charles made his court as French as he dared. He found that the upper classes in England (despite the grumblings of the mob) would take a great deal from France—etiquette, standards of taste, music, and a new sparkling wine called champagne. Would they, he wondered, take the French system of an absolute king?

It might be done, he reckoned, if Louis backed him and gave him enough money, from the deep coffers of France, to govern England without needing to call Parliament.

With his sister's help he planned the secret Treaty of Dover. When he judged the moment right, he was to announce himself a Roman Catholic. When Louis gave the word, England was to attack France's enemy, Holland. In return, Louis was to keep him well supplied with gold.

Minette got her husband's permission to visit Charles for a few days at Dover, while these points were being settled. Brother and sister enjoyed one of the happiest weeks of their lives, for the secret conferences were well varied with court festivities of every sort. When, reluctantly, she had to go home, Charles sailed half-way across the Channel to snatch another hour or two of her company.

They never met again. Within the month Minette was dead, after a sudden attack of peritonitis. "I have loved Charles better than life itself," she murmured as her eyes closed. "My only regret in dying is to be leaving him."

"My grief for her is so great," said Charles a short while afterwards, "that I dare not allow myself to dwell upon it. I try so far as possible to think of other things."

Her death did not, of course, affect the treaty Charles had signed, unknown to anyone in England except a handful of his ministers. After waiting a year or two, he put the plan into action by coming out as Louis' ally against Holland and by announcing religious freedom at home, as a prelude to his own change of church. But at once the horse reared under him: the English people would not have such a policy. With a violent effort he regained his seat in the saddle, cancelled his measure concerning religion, broke his alliance, and made a separate peace with the Dutch.

He did not make the same mistake again. After that he got his own way as far as he could by subtle, indirect methods— rigging the parliamentary elections so as to get a majority of his own supporters and letting ministers take the blame for whatever proved unpopular. "The King can do no wrong." The tradition suited Charles well enough. Some wit hung a paper on the door of the bedchamber:

> "*Here lies our Sovereign Lord the King,*
> *Whose word no man relies on.*
> *He never said a foolish thing,*
> *And never did a wise one.*"

Charles took the joke with his usual urbane good-humour. "Quite true," he remarked, "for my words are my own—but my acts are my ministers'!"

Politically-minded men might attack his policies. They might elect—in spite of all his tricks—a Whig party majority which might force him to do this or that. But the people at large would never rise against this sportsman king who supped with the jockeys at Newmarket and was hail-fellow-well-met with every class of society. They remembered how he had stood amid the blazing ruins of London in the Great Fire of 1666, passing buckets with his own hands and scattering golden guineas to the demolition gangs. They remembered how he had taken command of his troops when the Dutch fleet had sailed up the Thames and threatened the city. They remembered how, when the mutinous sailors rioted in the Strand, he had ridden into their midst and so pacified them that they gave him three lusty cheers before they dispersed. Yes, King Charles was all right. . . .

He kept them in that mind for a quarter of a century, and could have done so longer. But in February, 1685, the end came suddenly. Charles had a seizure as he was getting up, one morning. For several days he lingered between life and death, suffering agonies—more from his doctors even than from his disease—yet never losing the courage, the humour, and the thoughtfulness for others which had always marked him. He apologised to his lords for being so long a-dying. More seriously, he begged the Queen's pardon for all his shortcomings to her. On the last evening a Roman Catholic priest was smuggled into his room in disguise and Charles was received into the church which was his mother's, his brother's, and his wife's.

Towards dawn he murmured: "Open the curtains that I may once more see day." They did so. Gradually the winter light grew stronger. He was never to see it fade. Just before twelve he slipped out of the world he had loved so ardently, and James II was King.

The faithful, wicked old Chiffinch was with his master to the end. He was still Page of the Backstairs at the ripe age of eighty-two, still friend and keeper of the King's secrets. But the secrets of death were something he could not share for a few years longer. Charles had passed through a private door, of which even Will Chiffinch was as yet denied the key.

7

William III: The Dutch General

"About ten at night the Prince came home, and we found an easy admission. His attendance very inconsiderable as for a Prince; but yet handsome, and his tutor a fine man, and himself a very pretty boy."

So wrote Mr. Pepys in his diary at the Hague, in May, 1660. On the following day he was to see and kiss the hand of his new sovereign, Charles II. Amid all the excitements of the Restoration it could scarcely have entered his head that, within those few hours, he had seen two other future kings of England—not only Charles's younger brother James, but his nine-year-old nephew, then Prince of Orange but one day to be crowned William III.

Pepys was right in noting that his "attendance" was "very inconsiderable". Despite his princely rank and ancient family, the boy counted for little in Holland. The country was a prosperous middle-class republic. There was no court. Nothing to compare with the stately splendour Englishmen remembered from the days of Charles I and most certainly nothing to hold a candle to the dazzling glories of the Sun King, Louis XIV, at Fontainebleau.

"The Hague is a most neat place in all respects," wrote Pepys. *"The houses so neat in all places and things as is possible."* Not very descriptive—yet in that one word, "neat", he had struck the keynote. The whole country was as neat and regular as one of its own tulip-fields. Efficiency, cleanliness, progress, invention . . . those were the qualities in which Holland was leading Europe. The very land had a geometrical straight-

ness: without those long horizontals of embankment and canal, much of Holland would have been lost beneath the untidy sea.

Pepys was not perhaps quite so accurate when he described William as "a very pretty boy". True, the young prince had inherited some of the Stuart features from his mother—the dark almond eyes, the reddish-brown hair, the full mouth in the oval face—but he had been delicate from birth and was never exactly glowing with health. Time was to tighten those full lips and narrow those dark eyes, until sometimes they would close completely for an instant, under the pressure of the aching cares in the brain behind. Smallpox would come, and mark a skin toughened by wind and rain and the smoke of many battles. These changes were to come later, but even at nine William was by no means the ideal of a healthy, care-free small boy. Pepys, however, was too much of a snob to admit, even in his most private diary, that one of princely rank could be anything but "very pretty".

William had never known his father, who had died of smallpox eight days before the boy was born. William had therefore been brought up mainly by his mother, who had supervised his early lessons just as her own had been supervised by her conscientious father, Charles I. As Mary had been an English princess, William might very well have grown up with more knowledge of England, and affection for English ways, than he actually did. But Mary's mother had been French and her father had been the child of Scottish and Danish parents, so that she had no strictly English blood or at least only a few drops, much diluted down the years. Also, it was a long time since she had lived in England. She had been married in 1641, before the Civil War, though it was not until nine years later, on 4th November, 1650, that William was born. Until the day in 1660 when Pepys came over with the fleet to fetch back her brother to his throne, England had been no place for members of the Stuart family.

She saw that her little son was taught English, along with French and German, and he was an obedient pupil, though his English was never perfect and he could never get rid of his guttural Dutch accent. He learnt mathematics, too, and "military science", though it is a little difficult to imagine how much of the latter subject he could have understood during his mother's lifetime. For, a few months after the Restoration, when she was in England visiting Charles and sharing in the celebrations of his home-coming, she caught smallpox and died as her husband had done.

An orphan at ten, William faced the world alone.

Nor was it a very friendly world.

From his earliest years William had been taught about the special and peculiar position his family occupied.

He knew that his title came from nowhere in Holland but from a tiny pocket of independent territory in southern France. Orange was an ancient Roman town, with ruins of a magnificent theatre and triumphal arch, near to the River Rhône. William never saw the place, and its classical remains would scarcely have appealed to his severely practical mind. Orange lay deep in France which, throughout his life, was hostile territory, even during those years when there was no open war.

The title had come into William's family, the Nassaus, more than a hundred years before. Much more important to them, though, was another title—that of Stadtholder, or chief magistrate in the Dutch Republic, which had been voted to them for ever.

The Dutch Republic had come into existence, in the previous century, when the people drove out their Spanish masters. Among William's earliest impressions were the faded Spanish standards which hung, trophies of victory and national liberation, in the great hall of his palace at the Hague. That palace, like the post of Stadtholder, had been given to his family for their outstanding leadership in bygone days. William might be proud to know that his ancestors included the ancient kings of England and Scotland: he was probably even more proud that, on his father's side, he was the descendant of Holland's hero, William the Silent.

Bygone glories were all very well. But the orphaned boy, pacing sadly through the lonely galleries of his moated palace, or riding, without brothers or sisters or close friends, through the oakwoods outside the town, must have wondered how he would ever be able to live up to them.

His mother, on dying, had appointed her brother, King Charles, as his guardian. But Charles, far away in London. had other matters to think about. William was left to grow up at the Hague, the Dutch government paying his household expenses but not showing any great interest in his future —if indeed he had one.

The Dutch (the boy realised, as he grew older) saw no further need for the House of Orange which had led them to independence. Strictly, the country was a republic, known as the United Netherlands to distinguish it from the Spanish Netherlands, which are now Belgium and Luxemburg. It was governed by a body known as the States General, representing the various provinces, of which "North Holland" and "South Holland" were only two. There was no reason why the "presidency", or office of Stadtholder, should be reserved for the Princes of Orange. Oliver Cromwell, indeed, had bullied the Dutch into voting that it should *not* be. If Charles II did nothing else for his nephew, he had at least got them to alter that and to give back to William the office held by his forefathers.

In certain ways—not only their republican form of government but their business man's outlook and their tremendous enterprise—the Dutch in that century had a good deal in common with the Americans of today.

William realised that the heart of Holland beat not in the quiet Hague (except for a few days now and then when the

States General met in solemn assembly) but in the bustling Exchange of Amsterdam, thirty miles to the north. Like Venice, Amsterdam was a city built on piles amid the swamps; it was now the biggest and wealthiest city in Europe.

Holland might be small, no more than half the area of Wales, but she was immensely rich. The Bank of Amsterdam was the financial centre of Europe, as the Bank of England was to be, later—indeed, the Bank of England was founded in William's reign, with help from the Dutch institution.

William never forgot he was a prince. His own interests and enthusiasms were princely: he was a horseman and a hunting man, a soldier and a statesman. He had his own opinions about the hardheaded bankers and merchants who ran the affairs of his country while he was a boy; but, as a Dutchman, he could hardly fail to be proud of that country's position in the world.

He saw the Dutch East India Company's fleets sailing to the ends of the earth and bringing back fabulous cargoes. He knew that Dutch shipbuilders had no superiors in Europe. Dutch cattle were the best. Dutch farmers led the way in everything. They were the first to grow fields of turnips, potatoes, clover, and other crops for winter-feed; they were already famous for their dairy produce. It was the same with market-gardening and ornamental gardening: the Dutch tulip was renowned wherever men talked of flowers. Holland was celebrated for her fabrics and her porcelain, her metalwork and her diamond-cutting, and a variety of other skills.

Her citizens might be business men, but they cared for culture. Some Dutch portrait-painters might cross the North Sea to seek their fortune at the English court, but most artists found plenty of commissions at home. The University of Leyden ranked higher among scholars than either Oxford or Cambridge, and it was said that more books were published in Holland than in the rest of Europe put together. Both printing and engraving were far ahead of English standards.

William had no cause to feel inferior because he had been
born in the small country of Holland.

What was more to the point was the question, how could
he restore his family's position in a republic which felt no
need of him?

Another blow fell upon him in the year of his mother's
death. King Louis decided to mop up the patch of independent
territory in the midst of his kingdom. His troops invaded
Orange and dismantled the fortifications. More than ever,
now, William's title "Prince of Orange" had an empty
sound.

The real power in Holland, all this time, was the Pensionary,
or chief minister, Jan de Witt. His supporters called him
"the Wisdom of Holland". There was a feud between the
de Witt family and the House of Orange—Jan's father had
been imprisoned by William's—and so long as Jan, and his
brother Cornelius, controlled affairs, the boy knew that
nothing would be done to restore his fortunes.

It was de Witt who had the last word in his upbringing,
until he was of full age. William learnt to keep his thoughts
to himself. He had little interest in sports and games—riding
and hunting were the only kind of exercise he enjoyed—and
there were few chances of friendship with other boys, though
there was one, Jan Willem van Bentinck, two years older than
himself, who remained his trusted companion for the rest of
his life. Otherwise, William was very much of a lone wolf.
Like William I, six hundred years earlier, he had been born
to a troubled inheritance. He had to learn the lessons of
patience and craftiness, so as to survive the dangers around
him. The first essential was to reach manhood. When he
was a man, and no longer a boy, he would know how to
strike, and where.

He was nearly fifteen when war broke out with England.
An English fleet took possession of the Dutch colony on

Manhattan island, and its name was changed from "New Amsterdam" to "New York" in honour of the sea-loving Duke, William's Uncle James. The war was a naval one, wasteful to both sides, and the honours were about even. Peace was made after a couple of years, and the English ambassador, Sir William Temple, came over with a grand scheme for a Triple Alliance between England, Holland, and Sweden, the three great Protestant nations of northern Europe.

What a mistake, argued Temple, for such natural allies to fall out among themselves! They should unite against the real enemy, France, which, under the ambitious Louis, was seeking to dominate Europe.

Temple's suggestion appealed especially to the Dutch. They were by far the easiest mouthful for Louis to gobble up, for they alone had no sea between themselves and France, and all their warships were of no avail against the swarming masses of the French. De Witt welcomed the new alliance, and William, who differed on so many other points, entirely agreed on this. A united front against France was the object he worked for throughout his career.

Temple was to have a big influence on William's life—but not yet. De Witt, as Pensionary, was the man who mattered and the man he had to deal with. The Prince of Orange was only a powerless boy.

After the war with England was over, De Witt resumed his vendetta against the last survivor of the House of Orange.

An edict was passed, abolishing the office of Stadtholder. De Witt called upon William and told him he must quit the palace.

William retorted that it was his family-home and had been for generations.

True, admitted the Pensionary. But legally the palace was public property. As a matter of courtesy the Princes of Orange had been allowed to live in it, but now . . .

William considered. He had seen this struggle coming. Had the time come to make a stand? Was he old enough now to assert himself? If he let himself be turned out, would he ever regain his position? He knew the strength of De Witt and his supporters. How strong was the sentiment of the people for their princely house?

Long odds did not frighten him. He made his decision. If the States General wanted him out of his home, they would have to turn him out by force.

De Witt eyed the sullen, determined boy, and bit his lip. It was his turn now to take stock of the situation. Much as he wanted revenge for the humiliation his own father had suffered in days gone by, he saw that if he pressed this point he might overreach himself.

In the end, rather than risk a popular outcry in sympathy with the prince, De Witt and his supporters dropped the idea. William stayed on in the moated palace where the tattered Spanish banners drooped from the walls. He had won his own first little victory. And now he must not stand on the defensive, he must press his advantage. He was eighteen. Old enough, and ready, to fight.

Sir William Temple has left us a description of the Prince at this time: "*A young man of more parts than ordinary, and of the better sort; that is, not lying in that kind of wit which is neither of use to oneself nor to anybody else, but in good plain sense which showed application if he had business that deserved it; and this with extreme good and agreeable humour and dispositions without any vice; that he was asleep in bed always at ten o'clock; loved hunting as much as he hated swearing, and preferred cock-ale before any wine.*"

William, in short, was just the type of young man that any worthy, God-fearing merchant in Holland would have welcomed as a son-in-law. His religious views, his habits, his tastes, had nothing in common with those over-gay

Stuarts across the water in wicked London. In all that was known about him there was no cause for alarm.

His first move was to appear before the public assembly of Zealand, a province in the extreme south-west. Politely he reminded them that he had reached the age at which, in the past, they had always elected his forefathers "first noble" of the province. The Zealanders exchanged glances, debated, and then decided to maintain the family tradition. William had privately hoped that they might go further and choose him as their own stadtholder, but they did not. Still, he had made a beginning. The position of "first noble" entitled him to a seat in the States General, as representative of the Zealand nobility.

Two years later, in his twentieth year, William paid his first visit to England. It was no difficult journey in time of peace—London and the Hague were closer, in travelling time, than London and York or London and Exeter. The English capital was full of Dutch business men, clustered round their own church at Austin Friars; and there were many Dutchmen settled in outlying counties such as Devon and Cambridgeshire.

William would not have felt a stranger in a strange land, if his visit had been spent in these circles. But in England he was very much the Prince of Orange and a Stuart. London gave him a civic banquet, Oxford an honorary degree, but for the rest of the time he was mainly at Whitehall, breathing what he felt to be the tainted air of his uncle's scandalous court. He viewed his uncles with suspicion. James, of course, was an open Roman Catholic. Charles he was not sure of—but if that cynical, worldly monarch had any religious leanings at all, William guessed that they tilted the same way. He was over-fond, too, of the French . . . How far, the Prince wondered, could he be trusted to support this Triple Alliance against Louis, for which his own ambassador had worked so hard?

During this visit William met his cousin—"she-cousin", as Pepys would have termed her—the eight-year-old Mary, James's elder daughter. A pretty, sweet-natured child, she was not often to be seen at court; which was just as well, William grimly concluded, at her tender age. She lived mostly at Richmond Palace, in the care of Lady Frances Villiers, who had a tribe of children of her own. William was glad to find that her father had not been allowed to influence her towards his own creed: Parliament insisted that Mary, as a possible heiress to the throne, must be brought up in the Church of England. Her chances of wearing the crown might be small—the Queen might yet have a child, or James's new second wife from Italy might have a baby boy to displace his half-sisters in the order of succession— but every possibility had to be considered. With Europe divided into two camps by religion, the faith held by the ruler of England was no private matter but a life-and-death political question to millions.

So, noting his uncles' inclinations—the one open, the other masked and doubtful—William looked with hope and interest at his little cousin. Perhaps some day, if all went well, they would be allies in the cause, she Queen of England and he Stadtholder of the United Netherlands. It is most unlikely that another possibility ever entered his mind at this stage, that one day they would be also husband and wife.

That was 1670. William returned home, and in little more than a year his worst suspicions about his Uncle Charles were confirmed.

In 1671, as related in the previous chapter, Charles signed the secret Treaty of Dover with the French king. Though William knew nothing of this at the time, his shrewd eye began to note signs of the approaching storm. The English ambassador was recalled—that good friend of Holland, Sir William Temple, who had dryly summed up King Louis as "a great comet, expecting not only to be gazed at but admired". And Temple had been so disgusted by whatever he had found out on his return to London that he had resigned and retired into private life. Evidently something was brewing which Temple disagreed with, and that something was unlikely to be to Holland's advantage. In Sweden, too, where an inefficient council of regents was governing the country for the boy king, Karl XI, the French were using bribes to break up the northern alliance.

De Witt had been slower than William to see these danger-signals. He had trusted not only Charles (which was understandable) but Louis also, though France was the obvious enemy. Louis had flattered him, agreed about the House of Orange, and congratulated him on keeping the young Prince out of power. De Witt had many good qualities, but, when the Orange family was mentioned, he lost all sense of balance. To him, the young man at the Hague must always be the real adversary, not any king in Paris or London.

But at last even De Witt saw the storm which was about to burst. He asked Louis the meaning of various warlike preparations. He was told, blandly, that he would know in the spring.

War with France was coming, obviously. Only if Dutchmen of all parties closed their ranks could the enmy be beaten back. William the Silent could have led them to victory. Could his great-grandson do so now?

De Witt yielded reluctantly to the people's demand. William, now just twenty-one, found himself appointed Captain-General of the Dutch forces. There was not a day to lose. He began to examine the resources at his disposal, and as he did so his face took on an even grimmer look than usual. The De Witts had shockingly neglected the defences. Veteran troops had been disbanded, officers had grown slack in their duties, important commands had been put in the hands of mere civilians.

William himself had had no first-hand experience of war,

WILLIAM III

but all his young life he had been keenly interested in strategy and fortification. He had toughened his own weak body by riding and hunting, which he thought of as training for cavalry-warfare. With sufficient time, and a free hand, he knew he could reorganise the army—but he had neither. De Witt had managed to hamper him by getting all sorts of petty conditions and restrictions attached to his appointment; and he was only to hold it for a year.

In his blacker moods William may have wondered whether he had been right to accept it at all. Was it a trap, a trick of De Witt's to discredit him with the Dutch people? Suppose Holland could not stave off the French attack. Who would be blamed for her surrender—William, the general commanding her armies, or De Witt, the minister who had previously neglected them? Was De Witt more anxious to defeat the King of France—or the Prince of Orange?

In that spring of 1672 the storm burst. England declared war on Holland, and France sent her armies swarming over the Dutch frontier as remorselessly as a flood-tide from the North Sea. The defences went down like sand-castles. Large garrisons hauled down their flags without firing a shot. De Witt, seized with panic, proposed surrender.

Then occurred one of those extraordinary national upheavals which sometimes convulse a people in the hour of disaster, when the man in the street is braver, in his ignorance of the odds, than the government sitting in council with the hopeless facts before them. And when, in the end, the ignorant man in the street is proved to be right.

All eyes turned to the Prince of Orange. At Dordrecht, the historic town where the Dutch had held their first assembly after driving out the Spaniards just one hundred years before, there was a great demonstration in his favour. The magistrates met and revoked their previous edict which had ended his position as Stadtholder. The news was carried from city to city. Hurried meetings were called. In one place after another, William was voted back into his family's traditional office. The States General came together and solemnly confirmed the people's verdict. De Witt and his brother Cornelius were denounced as traitors. They were saved once from assassination, but soon afterwards the mob raided their prison, dragged them out, and savagely lynched them in the street. William shed no tears over his dead enemies. He had other matters to occupy him.

Holland had risen as one man, to repel the invader and wipe out the disgrace of those first surrenders. As one man? Even the women and children flung themselves into the struggle. In front of Ardenburg they joined with their men-folk—a mere two hundred citizens and a hundred soldiers—and held back a French force estimated at five thousand. At Groningen the university students manned the defences along with the townsmen, and boasted that they had withstood thirty thousand besiegers. Some reports might be exag-gerated, but of one thing there was no doubt: William's leadership had stirred up a new spirit in the land.

Was spirit enough, he wondered, against the sheer weight of the invading hordes? Louis had sent a hundred and twenty thousand men into Holland. The Dutch, unsurpassed at sea, could not possibly muster enough land-forces to hold them. The French were what the Spaniards had been a century before, the finest soldiers in Europe. But whereas Spain had been far away and reinforcement difficult, France was near and therefore more dangerous. Would captured French banners ever hang beside the faded Spanish trophies at the Hague?

The French banners nearly did reach the Hague—but if they had done so, they would have flown over the palace in triumph, not drooped indoors. The Dutch had resorted to their traditional method of defence: they had breached the dykes, and let the sea flood great stretches of the country. This held up the enemy at first, but when the water froze they were able to advance across the ice. They would have reached the Hague if there had not been a sudden thaw.

Still, the war had not proved as simple as Louis had expected. He and Charles offered terms. Charles, in particular, had only goodwill for his nephew personally: it was De Witt that Charles had disliked, and with De Witt gone and William in power, he would have been only too glad to get out of a war which his own subjects hated. He suggested that William should become the sovereign ruler of Holland, protected and guaranteed by Louis and himself.

William rejected the offer scornfully. He would rule Holland as the elected Stadtholder of the Dutch people, but he had no desire to be forced upon them by their foreign enemies.

"I will never betray the trust of my country, that my ancestors have so long defended," he declared. If need be, he would "die in the last dyke". He urged the States General to continue the war. Even if the country were overrun, they should take ship and maintain the struggle from their East Indian colonies. So, in 1672, William set the example which was to be followed by the Dutch Government after the German invasion of 1940.

It did not come to that, for William. He held on to a good deal of territory, fighting the French with dogged determination while, at sea, his admiral De Ruyter gave the English fleet rather more punishment than he received. William meanwhile was learning to be a general. He took several towns and failed to take others—he was sound rather than brilliant, but his men were quick to note that he took care of them and threw no lives away uselessly. If he had to retreat, he had the knack of doing so with the minimum of loss to his own army and the maximum to its pursuers.

Only with his own life was he ever careless. In the third summer of the war he fought a day-long battle at Seneff against the famous French commander, the Prince of Condé.

The casualties were heavy on both sides, but the result doubtful. Condé remarked afterwards, admiringly, that William behaved throughout the day like a veteran general except in one single respect: he always exposed himself to fire like a rash recruit.

There was no doubt that William loved soldiering. He was never so happy as when he was living the hard life of the camp.

The year after Seneff he caught smallpox, the curse of his age, and of his own family in particular. For a few days his followers held their breath. William was now the one hope of their country. They had made him Stadtholder for life, they had voted the office perpetually to his sons and grandsons after him. Was he to die now, as both his parents had died before him—but, unlike them, unmarried and leaving no heir to carry on the House of Orange?

William recovered. The war went on. Gradually, for all the heroic resistance of the Dutch, the superior weight of the French was beginning to tell. William realised that it was not enough to be a general, he must be a statesman too. He could never hope to beat France. Sooner or later he would have to make terms, and rather worse terms than he had wished for. His duty to Holland was to get the best terms he could.

First he would go for the weak point in the grouping against him. The English people were half-hearted about a war they had never wanted, and they had forced Charles to make a separate peace with him after two years. Now was the time to bring Holland and England back into their old friendship, and link them in a way which no secret plottings between Charles and Louis could break.

William decided to marry his cousin Mary, who was now fifteen.

Choosing a good moment, when both Charles and his chief minister Danby were in difficulties, he arranged a state visit to London. Charles was obviously anxious to see the long-drawn-out war between France and Holland brought to some conclusion. He wanted William to accept reasonable terms and was quite willing to offer his niece in marriage as an inducement. William was a firm bargainer, however. Marriage first, he insisted. Then he would discuss the peace. If one had to trust the other, he preferred that Charles should trust him.

Charles shrugged his shoulders and agreed, James (the girl's father) flew into a passion but obeyed the King, Mary* dissolved into floods of tears, and Louis, when he heard the news, took it "like the loss of an army". The calmest actor in all this drama was almost certainly the bridegroom himself.

There was one more summer of fighting after that. On the 11th August, 1678, the States General accepted (while William was absent at the front) a peace with France on worse terms than he had confidently expected to get after his visit to England. Three days later—before official dispatches had reached him from the Hague—he won a major victory over the French at Mons.

It was too late to make any difference. Messengers arrived while the dead were still being buried. The war was over.

William was now a man in his late twenties, a man's man with gruff ways and no graces, serious, care-worn, old beyond his years.

Mary was in her middle 'teens, young even for her age and unsophisticated, frivolous in her tastes—dancing and acting and card-playing, even on Sundays—yet with it all surprisingly innocent and unspoilt by the English court-life from which she had been so suddenly snatched.

They were an ill-assorted couple. But the marriage, which had begun so unromantically, turned out surprisingly well.

Mary fell in love with this dour, tight-lipped stocky

---

* The story of this wedding is told more fully in *The Seven Queens of England* as it meant more to Mary than to William.

soldier, whom another Englishwoman, Celia Fiennes, was soon to describe in her journal as "*our Hero King William III tho' little in stature yet great in achievements and valour*". She fell in love, too, with Holland and the new home which he had prepared for her, the lovely Palace in the Wood, surrounded by the oak-forests outside the Hague.

Mary was essentially a home-loving person, and that was just what William needed. He did not want a politically-minded wife who would expect to discuss every problem with him. When he came home, from council chamber or military camp, he preferred to relax.

An orphan since his tenth year, he had known so little home-life. Mary gave him a quiet happiness he had never before enjoyed. He was not good at showing his feelings— years of hiding them from De Witt and other enemies had made him reserved, and he was too old now to alter his ways. But, though he could not match Mary's open-hearted devotion to himself, he developed a deep affection for her which grew stronger every year.

The marriage had been made for political reasons, and, though it became more and more a genuine human marriage of two people, it did not lose its political importance.

There was peace, now, with France, but William had no illusions. Some day the unfinished struggle with Louis would be resumed. Meanwhile, he must gather the allies he had lacked before. Sweden, the German princes, even the Catholic emperor in Spain. Anyone, in fact, who would resist Louis' ambition to be master of Europe. England was vital to William's plan of defence, but England, under Charles II, was always the doubtful factor.

She became even more doubtful when Charles died and James II succeeded him. Though James had become (most reluctantly) William's father-in-law, eight years ago, all his sympathies were with Catholic France.

William began to watch affairs in England very carefully.

His wife was heiress to the throne. Her younger sister Anne came next, and he himself was third in line, as a grandson of Charles I. He was not interested in England for its own sake, but only as an essential piece in the jigsaw puzzle of defence against Louis. The completion of that jigsaw was the work Fate had given him, and all his life was directed to it.

Two years after James's accession, he sent over a trusted emissary, Dykevelt, officially as ambassador, but actually to spy out the land, make contacts with English statesmen, and remind them that, in case of need, the rightful heiress to the crown was the Princess of Orange, just across the North Sea.

James was already showing, by his tactless and dictatorial behaviour, how shrewd his brother had been in prophesying that he could easily lose his throne. It took James barely two years more to prove Charles completely right.

In the spring of 1688 William received a visitor at the Hague. He was Edward Russell, nephew of the Earl of Bedford. He brought a long tale of complaint about the King's actions in trying to force his own religion upon the country.

Russell ended by urging William to invade England with an army, in the defence of "the laws of England and the Protestant religion".

William, wary as ever, would not promise anything. He could only come, he said, if invited by the principal men in the kingdom. At the back of his mind, too, was the knowledge that if he left Holland with any large force, Louis might seize his chance to declare war. However critical the situation in England, he must not leave his own country undefended.

That summer events moved swiftly.

First came the famous "trial of the seven bishops" who had made a stand against James. They were acquitted amid wild scenes of rejoicing. Within a day or two William held in his hands the invitation he had asked for—signed in code by Lord Shrewsbury, Lord Devonshire, the Bishop of London, and other key-men in the opposition to James.

A week later came very different news from England. After years of childless marriage, a baby son had been born to James and his second wife. William's face darkened. This baby altered the whole line of succession. Mary, Anne, himself, they were all three out of the running . . . James, one could depend upon it, would have this child brought up to his own ideas, not those of Parliament.

If William was ever for a moment insincere in his religious observances, it was surely at that moment when he knelt in his private chapel at the Hague and muttered "Amen" to the new prayer added to the service on behalf of the royal baby. There was an added bitterness in the thought that he and Mary had been childless all these years, and there was no heir to the House of Orange.

More news came winging its way across the North Sea. Astounding rumours were circulating in London. That the new-born infant was not the child of the King and Queen at all, but one that had been smuggled into the palace in a warming-pan . . . that an elaborate plot had been made to cheat the English people by introducing a false prince, since no real one existed, so that Mary could be robbed of her rights to the throne.

William's brow puckered as he read dispatch after dispatch from his friends and agents across the water. Everyone there seemed to be convinced that the rumours were true. Even Princess Anne had reluctantly come to the conclusion that her father and stepmother had joined in a plot against her sister and herself. All kinds of circumstances were highly suspicious. It was altogether too lucky a coincidence for the King that, after all these years, he should suddenly be blessed with a son and heir when he most needed one.

Nowadays most people believe the baby was really the child of the King and Queen, and the warming-pan story is dismissed as propaganda. But it was widely accepted at the time, and William and Mary—with only their friends in England to guide them—had a good excuse to accept it. Did William truly in his heart believe it? That is something we shall never know. A man believes what he wants to believe. And if historians today still cannot feel absolutely positive of the facts in this case, William was certainly in no position to be sure at the time.

He had come to a turning-point in his life. If he did nothing now, made no sign, it would mean that he acknowledged the child as the next King of England. It meant a breach in the defence system against France which would never be filled in his own lifetime.

William began to muster ships and troops. Louis warned James, offered French forces, suggested that Portsmouth should become a French base in England. James, pig-headed and blind to his danger, was only aware that such French interference would stir his unruly subjects still more hotly against him: he refused the offer. Louis shrugged his shoulders, and, having schemes of his own afoot, sent his armies off to invade Germany. That was the best news William had heard for a long time. It was safe to leave Holland now; the way was clear to England.

In October he issued a manifesto, listing the various ways in which King James was flouting the laws of England. The sole object of his own journey was to ensure the calling of a free Parliament (just as General Monk had done before Charles II's restoration), so that a proper inquiry could be made into the true identity of the alleged prince. Once this was done, he would immediately withdraw his troops.

Six days after this manifesto, William made a farewell speech to the States General. He was not an emotional orator, but he deeply stirred his listeners. If there was a dry eye in the assembly, it was his own.

Two days later the States General voted to support his expedition. It was not, of course, a purely Dutch venture.

There were a good number of English exiles, ranging from William's political adviser, Dr. Burnet (afterwards Bishop of Salisbury), to Macclesfield and his troop of two hundred cavaliers on Flemish chargers. There were several organised English regiments which, by arrangement, had been lent to Holland. There was a Swiss Legion of fiercely bewhiskered soldiers of fortune and a band of Swedish knights in black cuirasses and cloaks of bearskin. And there was a force of Huguenots, French Protestant exiles recently driven from their own country by Louis' persecution.

It was an international crusade. It embodied the dream of William's life. His banner bore the words, *I Will Maintain the Protestant Religion and the Liberties of England*, but it was the first half, more than the second, which inspired his variegated host of volunteers.

He set sail on the day after the vote in the States General, but bad weather drove him back, and it was not till 1st November that his armada got finally under way. First, as a feint, he steered north as though to land in Yorkshire, then tacked and slipped through the Straits of Dover. James's fleet, under Lord Dartmouth, was held powerless in the Thames estuary by the same easterly wind which was blowing the invaders down the English Channel.

William was making for Torbay in Devon, but in the morning haze of 5th November he overshot his objective by several miles. It was a serious mistake. The next harbour along that rocky coast was Plymouth, and Plymouth was held by a man who would probably fight for James. By now, too, Lord Dartmouth might have worked his way out of the Thames and, once round the bend into the Channel, would be coming in hot pursuit. Luckily, at that moment, the wind obligingly changed. William was able to swing back into Torbay, and by noon he was ashore at the little fishing-village of Brixham.

For a week or two it was touch and go. The West Country

people were slow to join him. Their memories were too vivid of the earlier rising against James, three years ago, when the Duke of Monmouth's rebellion had ended in the Bloody Assizes before Judge Jeffreys, with wholesale hangings and sentences to slavery in the American plantations. Like an earlier William at Hastings, the Prince kept his line of retreat open and did not advance far inland during those first doubtful days.

But James was no Saxon Harold, and there was no further likeness between 1066 and 1688. Politicians, generals, whole regiments, began to trickle over to the invader. It became a landslide. As William gained confidence and began to push towards London through the southern counties, James found himself deserted by almost everyone—even his daughter Anne. He tried to escape overseas, but was recognised by some sailors and turned back. Next to James himself, William was the person most vexed by the sailors' zeal. He meant no personal injury to James, who, besides being his uncle, was his wife's father. If only James had got away, he would have saved his bacon and at the same time (as another English saying went) cooked his goose. His people would have little use for a king who ran away without making a fight of it.

By Christmas Eve William had reached the little Berkshire town of Abingdon, less than sixty miles from the capital. There, sitting in his billet in the Recorder's house, he received the best Christmas present he could have wished for—the news that James had made a second attempt, and this time had managed to leave the country. It was sweet news, more welcome even than those "sweetmeats upon treating the Prince of Orange" which still figure in the Corporation of Abingdon account-book, against the sum of £3 5s. 9d.

The "Glorious Revolution" had been accomplished without shedding a drop of blood.

.   .   .   .   .   .

Parliament met in the New Year. William was by then installed in London with his troops, but there was endless argument about the exact legal position. Had James II abdicated by fleeing to France? Should there be a Regent or a new sovereign? If a new sovereign, who? Obviously not the baby "prince", who was widely believed to be only a cuckoo in the nest. Then Mary, as next in line?

William put his foot down. He would not be Regent, nor would he play second fiddle to his own wife if she was made Queen. "No man can esteem a woman more than I do the Princess," he said bluntly, "but I am so made that I cannot think of holding anything by apron-strings. Nor can I think it reasonable to have any share in the government unless it be put in my own person, and that for the term of my life. If you think fit to settle it otherwise, I will not oppose you, but will go back to Holland and meddle no more in your affairs."

Mary wrote from the Hague supporting William. She was angry—as far as so gentle a creature could ever be angry —that the English were not warmer towards her beloved husband. She would not rule without him.

Grumbling, the Lords and Commons made the best of it. Princess Anne agreed to stand aside from second place, so that William, even in his own right, would rank next to Mary. On 12th February Mary arrived from Holland, and for once there were tears in William's eyes as well as her own when they were reunited. On the following day they were waited upon by a parliamentary delegation in the banqueting hall of the palace, and within a few hours the heralds were proclaiming them joint sovereigns as King William III and Queen Mary II.

So far, so good. But James had meanwhile taken heart. He was not beaten yet. In March came the news that he had landed in Ireland, backed by fifteen French warships and two or three thousand French troops. The Irish were of his own religion. They were rallying to him. He had entered Dublin

He had advanced into the northern, Protestant counties of Ulster, he was besieging Londonderry.

On the 19th April the English Parliament invited William to declare war on Louis whenever he thought fit. For once William almost beamed upon his counsellors. "This," he declared triumphantly, "is the first day of my reign!" His dream was taking shape.

He sent troops to Ireland under Marshal Schomberg, a veteran French commander who had been expelled for his Protestant beliefs and was now a trusted follower of William. But the Irish war dragged on, and after a whole year, in which he was tied to London by state business, William told Parliament he could delay no longer, he must go there himself. He appointed a committee of nine to advise Mary while he was away. She would get on well enough, for she understood these tiresome Englishmen better than he did. But for leaving her, he told Dr. Burnet, "I should enjoy the prospect of being on horseback and under canvas again. For I am sure I am fitter to direct a campaign than to manage your Houses of Lords and Commons!"

On 14th June he landed at Carrickfergus and took over command from old Schomberg. It was obvious to everyone that matters were going to move quickly now, and that soon there would be a decision one way or the other. "I haven't come to Ireland to let the grass grow under my feet," he told his men, as he issued brisk orders to prepare for action.

Two weeks later the two armies faced each other across the waters of the River Boyne. Occasionally the outposts exchanged a few shots, otherwise all was quiet. William, riding round to inspect the lie of the land, sat down on the river-bank to eat some breakfast. He was noticed and recognised, and two light field-guns were brought up by the enemy, in time to open fire as William remounted. One shot killed a member of his party, another ricocheted and grazed his shoulder, numbing his sword-arm. "No need for any bullet to come nearer," William admitted as the surgeon dressed his wound. Then he climbed stiffly into the saddle again and went on with his rounds until the midsummer dusk began to gather along the water's edge.

The next morning, 1st July, dawned fine. William took personal command of his own left wing, all cavalry, and attempted a difficult and dangerous river-crossing in the face of the enemy. Here James's Irishmen had a stiffening of French regulars, and it was old Schomberg the Huguenot who rallied the wavering attackers. "Come on, gentlemen!" he cried to his fellow-exiles in French. "Yonder are your persecutors!" The rival bands of Frenchmen went for each other murderously. Schomberg was shot and cut down by sabres. As the attack faltered for the second time, William battled his way across the river with his own Dutch guards and the Irishmen of the Inniskillen regiment. "Men of Inniskillen," he roared, "what will you do for me?" He pointed with his sword—he could scarcely strike with it, because of his wound. The men spurred after him through the blood-stained ford. The defenders broke, and James, watching from the safety of a hill-top, took his place at last at the head of his men—along the Dublin road, to safety.

For William, other battles remained to be fought, but on the continent of Europe. For nearly twelve more years he was to continue his policy of uniting Europe against France. They were to be years of hardship and care. He would never really understand the English, never be popular—but when had he cared much for popularity for its own sake? The English were splendid as comrades on a battlefield, and that was where he wanted them. Their bickerings in Parliament and council-chamber he would bear with what patience he could.

He disliked London. The coal-smoke stifled him. He lived at Kensington to escape it, and he and Mary began to reconstruct Hampton Court as the kind of country-home they both loved. Her sudden death of smallpox, at Christmas, 1694, was a tragic blow. "I have never known one single fault in her," he cried out. "No one but I knew her true worth. From being the happiest creature on earth I am going to be the most miserable!" It was several weeks before he could bear to meet people normally and deal with public business.

Seven years later, one Saturday morning in February, he called for his horse at Kensington and rode off to hunt at Hampton Court. His horse stumbled over a mole-hill and he was thrown, fracturing his collar-bone. It was set by a surgeon, and he went home in a carriage, but the jolting of the vehicle displaced the broken bone, and complications set in. On 8th March, 1702, William died, and was succeeded by his sister-in-law as Queen Anne.

He was only fifty-one, and his shortish life had been a half-century of danger and struggle, in which never for one moment had he lost his courage or relaxed his determination. He had not lived to see the success of his plans. Louis remained the great threat to the freedom of Europe, though William had given him some hard knocks, including the recent capture of Namur which was described as "the greatest humiliation inflicted on Louis in his career of conquest". The great victories however—Blenheim and the rest—had been left for Marlborough to win during the next few years. But the foundation for those victories had been laid by the little Dutch general, who now slept for ever among the kings of England.